At One With
The Heart of Creation

At One With
The Heart of Creation

Reflections and Verse
on the Spirit Journey

by
John P. Cock
with
Lynda L. Cock

tranſcribe books

ISBN 0-9665090-4-8

Printed in the United States of America

Dedicated to Thomas Berry

A friend, mentor, and our candidate for the Peace Prize for All Species, including the human. As we tell people in Greensboro, he may not only be the wisest person to be born and raised here, but he may also be the wisest person on the planet as he continues to speak and write – at age 89 – about a transformed earth-human relationship.

other books by John P. Cock

• **Bending History:**
Reflections of a Religious Revolutionary (2004)
co-editor of the selected talks of Joseph W. Mathews

• **Our Universal Spirit Journey:**
Reflection and Verse for Creation's Sake (2002)
with foreword by Thomas Berry

• **Motivation for the Great Work:** Forty Meaty
Meditations for the Secular-Religious (2000)
with foreword by Thomas Berry

• **The Transparent Event:**
Post-modern Christ Images (2nd ed., 2001)
a book about the way life is – full of grace

• **Called To Be:**
A Spirit Odyssey (2nd ed., 2000), *memoir of a
mountain boy who becomes a citizen of the universe*

See on-line bookstores or e-mail
tranScribe-books@triad.rr.com
or go to Web page
www.johnpcock.homestead.com

Acknowledgments

Besides spirit guides now, throughout our lives, and throughout history, we thank the following who helped us with this book: son John for his editorial discernment; son Jeremiah for his technical support; and other colleagues and retreatants for their shared insights, especially David Pope.

Contents

Section Three: **Intercommunion**

Introduction

This spirit journey book is about the human *experience of communion* with the *power at the heart of creation* that motivates us to be *agents of intercommunion*.

The book stands on stories of old: creation always begins out of nothing in response to creative power. Even though the old stories of creation carry unique interpretations, the essential message is the same: creation is *very* good, no matter what. The old creation stories are thanksgiving narratives inspired by the power at the heart of creation.

Three Sections

Section one is about linking our understanding of creation and its interior power to our current human condition: the people of this planet are dispirited. Some even say we suffer soullessness. We are out of touch with *spirit*. Or as Mother Teresa said, after a trip to the USA, she'd never seen such an abundance of things and such a poverty of the spirit. Our major contradiction is not economic, political, or cultural – it is spiritual.

The evidence seems obvious: warring and terrorism continue evermore fiercely; we deny the atmosphere is in big trouble; we let the poor get poorer; global diseases run rampant; we squander the planet's resources; we become more provincial; materialism drives us. Sounds like a Hebrew prophet's litany that would have been followed by a woeful declaration of cause: "You people are out of touch with the way things work here in creation. No wonder you are dispirited and your souls languish.

You have lost touch with that which makes creation tick."

This then is the book's context: humankind is in a spiritual malaise and struggles to articulate the reasons why. As the above master image of the book says, we are on a *spirit journey* – whether we are seekers or not – even though most of us in this secular age find such a statement strange. We think and act as though we're primarily on a *personal journey*. Yet, the journey is not about "me as a person" but is about "me in relation with all others," human and non-human.

This is not enough said, however. The truth we are missing is that *spirit* happens in the relation between the other and me, or *spirit* happens in the relations of creation. Since creation is one big set of relations, *spirit* is happening all the time and everywhere, yet we are unaware of it most of the time. Putting it all together, we are on a spirit journey we are not very present to, thus our dispiritedness and growing planetary suffering at our hands.

In this section we explore *spirit's* presence in everyday life and the dynamics of the spirit journey.

In *section two*, the book's master image says our spirit journey is about *our experiences of communion with the power at the heart of creation.* How do we begin to deal with *the* contradiction of our time which is spirit disrelation?

Answer: we become more aware of our experiences of communion with *spirit.* This section is out to help us understand that the cure is always at hand because communion is the way creation works. The title for the book applies here especially: *at one with the heart of creation.* In this section we illustrate experiences of communion that reunite us to the heart of creation through the particulars of creation, giving us new perspective and sometimes changed lives.

In *section three*, this spirit journey book talks about

the *power at the heart of creation that motivates human-kind to be agents of intercommunion.* Here the focus is the mission of creation as mutual care or *inter-communion.* In some ways this uncommon word is the same as *communion,* but we will use it more as a way to talk about our resolve and action to comprehensively interrelate with and care for creation as it cares for us.

Format and Our Intent for the Reader

The Reflections start as more experiential and move toward more interpretive as each of the three sections progresses. The Verses are meant to give tangential expression to the Reflections and add space for a more interior dialogue with the message at hand. Though there are some participatory exercises, this is not a workbook but rather a book with various reflective dimensions.

The intent of the book is to allow the reader the opportunity for brooding about creation and one's depth relationship with it. The word "deep" is showing up everywhere these days: deep ecology, deep time, deep space, deep structure, deep listening, deep mind. This tells us that cosmologists, physicists, psychologists, and other secular professionals are recognizing there is interiority in every discipline and that every particular of creation – in form and event – is full of depth.

Our intent is therefore twofold: point to the depth dimension/dynamic in creation and our lives, and, second, create a dialogue wherein communion and intercommunion become more conscious and may even happen; for communion and intercommunion are happenings, finally, beyond the control of our mind and will. We can set the table and serve the meal and trust that *spirit* is present. If so, all around the table will be blessed and nourished by being connected with the deep meaning that is always

15

present now; and partakers will embody the spirit of the meeting as they go forth.

Use of the Word *spirit*

It is important that we say up front what we mean by the word "spirit." You have already noticed that we do not capitalize the word but put it in italics: *spirit*. Maybe to go with a capital "S" would lose secular readers who are leery of things metaphysical. We'll use the small "s" – except to begin a sentence – and italics, to differentiate from the ordinary use of "spirit": team spirit, her spirit is high, the spirit of the nation is at a low ebb. Some uses will be trickier, such as "spirit journey" and "spirit consciousness," but we will italicize "spirit" only when we are definitely talking about the awesome power at the heart of creation.

Aboriginal peoples of any land, tens of thousands of years ago, were in touch with the "great spirit." We are their descendants and like them have a sense after that which is not just synonymous with natural and human spirit. At the same time, ordinary spirit is a window onto depth *spirit*.

Our disclaimer with the use of the word *spirit* goes like this: we are not talking about a transcendent reality but a transparent reality. We are not talking about a god in our image that we refer to as he or she. We're talking about the depth dimension of humankind's relations with all creation as we live the spirit journey from birth to death.

During the last few hundred years, the human focus has been on *this* existence as the realm of meaning, or things "existential." The word has fallen on hard times, yet we still use it because it says to us that existence in all its pain and glory is full of meaning. Back in the 20th century we used modifiers to describe thinkers as atheistic existentialists (Satre) or Christian existentialists (Tillich).

16

We would like to be referred to as *spirit existentialists*, meaning we understand *spirit* as the power at the heart of existence and creation.

Being raised Judeo-Christian trinitarians, we understand that "Holy Spirit" points to the power at the heart of creation. "God" and "Christ" are never far from mind, and we feel we can meaningfully dialogue with any Christian. But our audience is *any* human being, and we have decided strategically to go with the word *spirit*. It is more universal and inclusive and is harder to make into a graven image or an anthropocentric idol.

We must move beyond "a best religious dogma," which divides peoples and even causes wars. Our intent is to start with experience, using non-dogmatic, dynamic language that is more universally acceptable. We borrow from Zen Buddhism, quantum physics, Jung, transpersonal psychology, earth-spirit ecology, the Hebrew-Christian bible, and other religions and spiritualities when we say

> spirituality is the experiential understanding that there are zillions of forms in creation but only one primal energy: at the heart of all forms and events in our universe, there is one power or *spirit* permeating all, allowing each to be holographic of and synchronistic with everyone and everything.

Again, we want to speak to *any* human being. We know this indented paragraph is quite theoretical. We trust the book's Reflections and Verse speak more to our common human experience of depth.

Not a Short-term Effort

When it comes to reversing the human spiritual malaise we referred to earlier, we understand this is not a short-term effort. We are reminded of the task of Moses to liberate his people and lead them to the promised land in about forty years. Maybe even more appropriate was the task of Abraham to father a big part of humanity, as the story goes. His project has taken some 4000 years and now is taking a new leap: we humans are considering care not just for ourselves, our institutions, or our species, but for creation. Such care was our calling in the original books of faith of the children of Abraham. What if we picked up on our original, assigned vocation of care for creation and stopped killing each other and our environs as we recklessly strive to fulfill ourselves on our person-centered journeys?

Unless we grasp the new story of who we are, persons on a great spirit journey with all creation, and rediscover our deepest source of power – *spirit* and not munitions – we will further dispirit and even annihilate each other and other species in this part of creation called planet Earth. We are writing about the motivation to live into a new era, knowing the time line is at least 40 to 4000 years (see Appendix C). We are writing about what it will take to reclaim the promised land of mutual care for creation, or intercommunion, born out of communion with the heart of creation.

The change we envision will not come from the ought of sustainability, will not come from more democratic governments, more economic prosperity, or a better educated populace. It *will* come from a more *conscious spirit journey of communion and intercommunion* of a growing *movement* of people around the planet.

May this book help us all to be a part of the great work of healing in our time as we would journey *at one with the heart of creation.*

JPC with LLC
Greensboro, NC, USA
November 2003

The Starting Point

Have You Experienced the Mystery?

> The fairest ["most beautiful"] experience we can have is the mysterious. . . . Whoever does not know it and can no longer wonder, no longer marvel, is as good as dead. . . . It was the experience of mystery . . . that engendered religion. **~Albert Einstein**, 1930 (*The Expanded Quotable Einstein*, p. 295)

EINSTEIN HAD NOTHING ON US as he contemplated the universe and pondered his life journey. He experienced the mystery just as the rest of us humans do.

That is why we have sub-titled this book *Reflections and Verse on the Spirit Journey*. All of us are on that journey because we've all been encountered by the mystery over and over and marveled at the wonders of our existence in creation.

As you read my list of mysterious encounters below, jot down *your* own experiences in the space under each that brings to mind an awesome experience you have had.

Watching my mother cry after losing a child soon after birth

Burying my favorite cat at age six and leading the service

Watching my kite almost go out of site

Driving my uncle's tractor on the farm for the first time

Swinging out on a grapevine and dropping over the swamp

Breaking my collarbone in first high school football game

Watching the Sun come up at an Easter service

Losing an eye when an RC Cola bottle exploded

Being cared for lovingly by my mother in the hospital

Kissing my girlfriend for the first time

Being in the presence of a great person like Frank Laubach

Dancing at the prom till my sportcoat was soaking wet

Singing my favorite music in a great choir at college

Walking in the moonlight with my fiancé

Proposing to her at my fraternity banquet

Landing my first real job

Participating nervously in my marriage ceremony

Making love the first time

Worrying about how to make it financially

Making my first hole-in-one at Bide-a-wee Golf Course

Pulling our first U-Haul and ruining the new car's engine

Hugging the dog as he jumped up in my arms after work

Lifting the umbilical cord from around son's neck

Hearing about the assassinations of my heroes

Visiting patients on the terminal ward

Protesting a social injustice and almost being fired

Attending a life-changing seminar

Being called to enter upon a great cause

Living in the ghetto with the people we were trying to help

*Reading **The Courage To Be** and being revived*

Avoiding death miraculously in an auto wreck

Responding to a great talk by Joseph Mathews

Giving thanks that the plane did make the runway in Tokyo

Being overcome by the poverty in Kathmandu and Calcutta

Living in Muslim and Hindu villages for several years

Coming down with malaria

Taking our son to emergency care in Jakarta

Hiding our sons from angered villagers seeking revenge

Getting a phone call in Medan that my father had died

Sitting in the moonlight and reflecting with a village friend

Flying down the verdant Shenandoah, returning from India

Fasting for three days

Seeing the movie "Gandhi" after living in India

Sending out our teenage son to Africa to help in villages

Driving through a snowstorm from St. Louis to Chicago

Taking a close friend to the psychiatric ward

Going back home again to live

Starting a business with fear and fascination

Watching hurricane Hugo go down Main Street

Hearing our son make a high school graduation address

*Reading Thomas Berry's **Befriending the Earth***

Writing my memoir

Participating in our son's marriage ceremony

Holding our first grandchild

Pulling our six-month-old granddaughter up Main Street in the red wagon; putting her in the bed with her 85-year-old great-grandmother; and watching them ooh and aah as they tenderly played with each other

Holding Mother's hand as she died

Moving close to our sons and grandchildren

Cuddling our little ones as we read them stories

*Reading Berry and Swimme's **The Universe Story***

Undergoing family marriage struggles

Attending a reunion with over 300 close global colleagues

Watching "Earth on Edge" on PBS television

Losing close friends to death and thinking about my own

Hearing that 100 million died in wars of the 20th century

Losing money when the markets fell

Experiencing deep angst after 9/11

Reading human population will have tripled in my lifetime

Being told by the doctor that I have glaucoma

Gazing at Mars, more clearly, after 70,000 years

Learning that we're going to have another grandchild

The list could go on and on, as anyone knows, for we all have experienced the mystery in small and profound ways as we have lived our lives.

Look back over your list of awesome encounters, reflect a few minutes, and, if you will, write a closing statement on the next page about your life journey with *the mysterious*, as Einstein calls it, that has encountered us over and over.

My Journey with the Mystery

Reflecting upon my many encounters with that mysterious power . . .

Section One

Heart of Creation

Spirit journey: the experience of communion with the power at the **heart of creation** that motivates us to be agents of intercommunion.

Reflection 1

Spirituality 101

BEING AROUND CHILDREN is surely one way to keep sharp theologically. Granddaughter Kaitlyn, almost five at the time, had developed quite a prayer life. She not only had a variety of meal prayers that she had learned at home, church, and at school, but she also prided herself in making up her own, as well as saying what she called her grandfather's prayer, the Fifth City Preschool meal ritual:

> *Food is good. Right? (Right!)*
> *Life is good. Right? (Right!)*
> *All is good. Right? (Right!)*
> > *What do you say? (It's okay.)*
> > *What do you say? (It's okay.)*
> > *What do you say? (It's okay.)*
>
> *Let us eat this meal on behalf of. . . .*
> *Let us feast.*

A rather profound affirmation of life.

Kaitlyn asked if she could tell me a story about God. Her dad, Jeremiah, had warned us that she was having some serious discussions about where God came from. She began, "God pro-che-ated everything in the world. He [we'll have to work on her anthropocentric language] made plants and animals from some special recipes. Then he made people. He made grown-ups first so that they could have babies. Then he made kids."

She continued, "No one knows who made God or who his mother was. It's a mystery. But that's okay. I'll give

27

you some clues." About that time her mother and little brother, Nolan, came, so we never got the clues.

She was a young theologian sharing her understanding of life. Children experience the deeps of life because they also live in this wonder-filled universe. They too create stories, myths, doctrines, and morals just as religion-makers before them. She was asking deep questions and creating her language that communicates what she understood about life.

Life is the great teacher. It reveals itself in the way life is, and is experienced by all. First, we experience life, then comes religious reflection, making us all theologians.

Or, we could say, first comes spirituality, which is often followed by religion.

Verse 1

Spirit Journey

spirit is always happening to us on its journey

spirit is always reconciling us to its oneness

spirit is always awakening us to its mystery

spirit is always enlightening us with its presence

spirit is always freeing us for its mission

spirit is always calling us to its great work

spirit is always fulfilling us in its abundance

spirit is always creating us by its power

spirit is always sustaining us on its way

spirit is always transforming us in its image

spirit is always reigning over us by its grace

Therefore
     all is one
     all is whole
     all is good
     all is blessed

~april 15, 2003

Reflection 2

spirit Consciousness

WE ACT AS THOUGH we have only a few spirit experiences in a lifetime. But this is to miss the depth and richness of our lives. Therefore, let us watch for the many spirit experiences we have each day.

Spirit experiences come in all shapes and sizes. Our lives are full of external happenings that set off internal crises that raise life questions that we have to answer and live with. For example, I stepped off a downtown curb one day without looking, was almost hit by a speeding car, fell back just in time, immediately thought about what could have happened to me, and for the next day or so was reflecting on my life, what I was doing with it and what I might do with it. In total, a real spirit experience.

Likewise, our lives are full of glorious happenings that set off wonder, that draw us into the sheer mystery of living. For example, grandson Nolan at four-years-old jumped the tiny creek at our nearby park. He shouted, "Dah Dah, did you see that? I didn't even step in the water!" That was a spirit experience for him, and for me as I watched his naturally wonder-filled response to creation. I got a picture of what it means to be like a little child in relation to the wonder of life.

Art is a reflection on life. A couple of movies recently set off spirit consciousness within me. One was *About Schmidt*, who in the opening scene sits for the last few minutes of his career in his office at the insurance company where he'd worked most of his life. I identified with the impact of that moment on him: What will *I* do now?

31

That was a spirit moment for him – and for me as I watched.

In the movie *Antwone Fisher* I watched Antwone as a young man look for and find his mother, who had left him as a baby. My spirit reflection at those scenes in the movie was a deep sense of thanksgiving for my own mother, who was there for me and loved me from the first day of my life, and even before I was born, and all the sacrifices that followed until my independence and beyond.

I believe our lives are full of significant moments that occasion spirit reflection, as we become conscious of what is really going on, what is really present, what we are really experiencing. We may need help here.

We were part of a group[1] that created a comprehensively descriptive chart about depth human consciousness. Four major arenas – mystery, consciousness, care, and tranquillity – were divided into sixty-four states of being, or states of awareness, and 576 poetic descriptions of the experiences of a conscious person. What we were after was a way to talk about all our life experiences as profound. We used the title "The Other World Charts,"[2] believing that the other world is in this world, or that *spirit* is at the heart of our living, whether we are deeply conscious of that presence or not. Such methods help persons become aware of their extraordinary-ordinary journeys with *spirit*.

Life's experiences call forth deep human responses and sensitivities. I deliberately try not to use psychological language here, because what I'm talking about is deeper. It's about our total experience of life, about what just *is* in every here and now of life, if we are given to see – if we are conscious of what is going on at a deeper level. To keep myself vigilant about my self-conscious spirit journey, I rehearse Kierkegaard's alarming quote:

> The greatest danger, that of losing one's own
> self [one's relationship with *spirit*, as he writes

throughout his works], may pass off quietly as if it were nothing; every other loss, that of an arm, a leg, five dollars, a wife, etc., is sure to be noticed. (*The Sickness Unto Death*, p. 165)

In order not to miss our lives, let's try some sort of daily ritual of picking and reflecting upon a few key events of our day, each day. Simple enough. And through simple multiplication, say 3 times 365 days of each year, realize that each one of us will have thousands upon thousands of self-conscious experiences during our life journey. Think such reflective consciousness will make a difference? Think it will change the way we see life, the way we live life?

Maybe we have lived long enough to realize that our life journey is a stream of events that wake us and keep us mysteriously and wondrously conscious. Could it be that we are *spirit*-conscious creatures by nature? I'd say *Yes*! and go on to say that our consciousness of *spirit* is our most human characteristic.

---

[1] The Order:Ecumenical/Ecumenical Institute:Chicago/Institute of Cultural Affairs. For more detail, read my memoir, *Called To Be: A Spirit Odyssey*.

[2] The charts are in print in Brian Stanfield's book, *The Courage to Lead*, pp. 106-13.

Verse 2

Lift My Spirit

I sit and wait for a movie to lift my spirit,
for it to prick and explode my illusions about life
and to leave me with a vision of new creation.

It surely doesn't have to be a box office hit,
a thing of violence so gruesome I scrunch in my seat,
nor so freaky or maudlin that I would want to leave.

It doesn't have to have famous stars or director,
the most sensational stage craft or outlandish price tag,
nor a blitz of TV ads coming at me for months.

Rabbit Proof Fence, Winged Migration, and *Whale Rider*
lifted my spirit as three sisters escaped the whites,
a species of nature soared, and a tribe was reborn.

And *The Pianist* uplifted me with his spirit,
surviving the devastations of war in his Poland
where once he was the artist of a dying order.

So you see, it doesn't take much to lift my spirit,
just a hour or two of a story of great life journey
responding to *spirit* from the heart of creation.

~september 14, 2003

34

Reflection 3

Teachers,
Please Ground the Truth

A LEADER OF A SUNDAY SCHOOL CLASS ordered copies of my *Motivation for the Great Work: Forty Meaty Meditations for the Secular-religious*. He and I conferred by e-mail several times before and during the sessions. One of my e-mails to him follows wherein I try to articulate the relationship between life experience and truth on the spirit journey:

Way to go,

I read every word of your lesson-plan and thank you very much for your time spent in preparing and sending them on to me. You are a theologian. Everybody is, for everybody makes basic assumptions about what is true for her/himself. However, some hide behind what the tradition of the scriptures says, what the tradition of the church says, what their family or close community say, or what the culture says. They therefore do not stand on their own authority and say, "Here I stand, this is what I believe out of my life experience." Instead, they too often proof text scripture and quote religious leaders.

An authentic theologian grapples with what s/he can believe is true for her/himself, but honors the other authorities that have made sense along the way. So, way to go, you are grappling with truth authentically, in most of what you sent me. That does not mean I agree with your take on the truth. Everybody's is a little different; therefore, dialogue can be very rich and helpful. Dialogue is necessary lest we think we know the whole truth and stop the spirit journey. And good dialogue allows for each person to articulate what s/he believes. If someone's articulation flies in the face of what I believe, that is good, for it calls to my attention what I believe or don't believe and helps me to figure out where I stand in my relationship with truth.

A kicker in all this is what we mean by the word "truth": do we mean rational truth or life truth, two very different things? Too often we spin our wheels dialoguing on rational truth, the truth of our ideas, rather than the truth that comes out of our life experience, or *grounded truth*, which comes out of our living, not out of our heads. How do we enable folk to struggle with life truth? is what my meditative Reflections are about.

That's the reason for the questions at the end of each of the book's forty Reflections. You notice that they are pushing the reader to talk about her/his life experience, where they have experienced this or that truth. If someone can't do that, they are ungrounded, abstract, don't know really what they're talking about. When Paul talked about loving Jesus and following him, he mentioned imprisonment, shipwreck, etc. He grounds what the abstraction of "discipleship" means. So, one of the first authentic responses to an abstract belief is what does it mean in my life experience. Have I been there or done that? If not, maybe I will be quiet and listen to someone else share a grounded experience. So, the Reflection questions are there to help us ground truth in our lives. This done, we will have a more authentic spoken dialogue among the group.

I would suggest, therefore, this simple format for the sessions: 1) have them read the most cogent paragraph or two of my printed Reflections, knowing all have not done so beforehand; 2) have them take a few minutes to answer the book's Reflection questions individually; 3) as a group, call on them to share grounded, life truth (what the tradition calls *witnessing* to each other out of one's life journey).

In the first instance, your sessions are not to find out what the author believes, or what you the group leader believes, but to find out what the participant believes from the heart, from grounded experience. Your job as the leader is to keep the participants sharing grounded dialogue, not abstract, secondhand beliefs. They are not there to sit and listen to your theology or my theology. They are there to discuss the truth, their reflections on the way life is for them. Even more, they are there to figure out where they stand in relation to truth and what "is the will of God," which all have to figure out for themselves, huh? My printed Reflections are simply a tool toward that end, I trust.

Do let me know how it goes.

Grace,

John

~may 22, 2001

Verse 3

That Which Wakes Us All

I'm not sure who woke up whom
this morning, the birds or I,
but awake we both are, sure
that there's something to wake up to

Their kingdom and mine are one
as we listen to and watch
each other's kindred spirit,
sensing there's that which wakes us all

~june 5, 2003

38

Reflection 4

Experience Your Experience

Experience is not what happens to you; it's what you
do with what happens to you.   **~Aldous Huxley**

If you are going to take care of yourself, every morning
not every other morning, you are going to get yourself
spiritually dressed. . . .

The first person to call my attention to the category
of *experiencing your experience* was a teacher of art
at the University of Texas years ago. . . . Later, I
understood it as grinding the spiritual meaning out of
every life situation, converting matter into spirit. And
from my meditation on that phrase I began to see how
much of a person's day goes down the drain of his one
unrepeatable life because he has not disciplined himself
to experience his experience, to stand at attention to
life. Look at the myriad of happenings that have
happened to us since we got up this morning. How
many did we embrace? How many did we bring into
our beings? Too few.

In Huxley's book (*Island*), the birds go around
crying, "Attention! Attention! Attention!" Then they say,
"Here and now! Here and now! Here and now!" You
stand at attention in life. You do not let one of those
episodes get by. . . . I warn you, you let one go by once
or twice or three times or four times or 450 times and
there may be no return. Some of you will fall flat on
your faces and then wonder what in the world caused
it. It was caused way back there when you let this or
that or the other reflection go by. And then you will
find yourself a great big hunk of shaking palsy and
will wonder, "Who out there caused this?". . . [W]ring

the profound meaning out of every situation. That is taking care of yourself.

Taking care of yourself has a great deal to do with not only prebrooding, but with what I call after-brooding. Nowadays, I think I am more interested in afterbrooding. . . . Your emotions are your means of standing at attention. If you are taking care of yourself, it is not just being delighted; you ask yourself why you are delighted. . . .

I would not pass anybody in the morning without saying "Good morning" or "Hello." I would not even dream of doing that. . . . The reason is simple: my passing you is my life. It has nothing to do with your life, in the first place. It is my life standing at attention.

. . . If you take care of yourself, you are going to need crutches, but you cannot take my crutches. You have to build your own: how you get up in the morning and how you maintain yourself through the day. These are not psychological crutches; they are spiritual crutches. . . . You are concerned with ways of [taking care of] your life. ~**Joseph W. Mathews** (1975 talk in forthcoming book, *Bending History*)

JOSEPH WAS ONE WISE MAN on a great mission. Our lives are one experience after another, whether we are somewhat reflective or deeply reflective.

Let me list experiences that come to mind just in the last couple of hours: waking to the song of the Cardinal, seeing the light of day, walking to the bathroom, walking back and doing my morning ritual, saying "good morning" to Lynda and giving her a hug, turning on the radio, fixing breakfast and eating together on the porch, looking at the trees outside, smelling the flowers on the table, stumping my toe as I go to do the dishes, getting a phone call from Nelson that Shakuntalah had just died in India and reflecting with Lynda on our wonderful times with her,

40

cleaning up, sipping my second cup of brew, hugging and chatting with my grandchildren who came by to leave a dessert, and writing this reflection up to this line – and on and on into the rest of this one day in my life.

We get born, we grow up, we work, we recreate and communicate, and we die. In between we dream and daydream, we break a collar bone and lose an eye, we make love, we give birth, we move over twenty times, we have great adventures of service around the world, we feel, we think, we remember, we laugh and cry, we breathe. All these experiences, and our reflections upon them, are our very lives, whether we are thankful for them or not.

To make this most complex process more possible to think about, let's say we experience our experience in four steps: *experience, reflection, interpretation,* and *integration.*

1. Experience: I will take, for example, our *hearing of the death of Shakuntalah.*

2. Reflection: It was an awkward phone conversation with Nelson, full of noticeable pauses and breathing, wondering what to say next at such a time to her second father, who was trying to keep from breaking down.

3. Interpretation: Next came Lynda's and my remembrances of Shakuntalah's life and our time with her as we all did comprehensive village development together in India, and her several visits with us in Virginia and North Carolina. We shed tears as we rehearsed our relationship with her and the last couple of years of her heroic struggle with cancer, and especially how she never stopped doing her mission with Indian villages. Nelson and Elaine had just visited her and her husband in India and two days ago had sent a custom card made with two photos of her on their visit. On the front of the card she is being carried on a seat on the shoulders of four men. She looks like a beaming princess. The printed message by Nelson and Elaine inside recounts her last year with cancer, the current status of her mission in the villages, and thanks those who have helped with the costs of her treatment. I was especially struck by the lines, as we reread it just now, "Her spirit is consistently high. Both she and Shankar [her husband] have a positive attitude toward each other and life itself. She continues to be an inspiration to her doctors and everyone she meets." Lynda and I summed up our conversation with this deeper reflection, or interpretation: she understood her life to be an instrument for village renewal, dedicated to directly empowering thousands of villagers in the state of Maharashtra, India, and all the others around the globe that she encountered or who knew of her work. Her life was a gift from creation and a gift to creation.

4. Integration: We have been left with a sign of life lived on behalf of others. We have been touched by her spirit and her devotion to her mission. We will never be the same because of her living in our presence and in our memory. We are remotivated to live on behalf of others as we write this in remembrance of her fulfilled spirit journey.

Through these four steps, we just now *experienced our experience* of hearing of Shakuntalah's death. Experiencing our experience self-consciously makes a profound difference for our living fully. The self-conscious life is a hallmark of humanness. As Joseph says, "Wring the profound meaning out of every situation. That is taking care of yourself," or that is what it means to be deeply human. We can claim this moment in time or we can throw it away. We can live experiences to the hilt or we can waddle un-self-consciously through our lives and miss the living of them.

Experiencing our experiences takes practice, it takes discipline, Joseph says. Some simple spirit practices follow.

To begin the day, we need a verbalized *wake-up ritual*. One that we use comes from the Judeo-Christian tradition, "This is the day that the Lord has made; let us rejoice and be glad in it." If we rehearsed that type of wake-up ritual daily, would it make a difference? It would beat thinking about the things we have to do today – or trying to think of something to do today – and becoming overwhelmed or forlorn. Instead, we can give thanks for the day we have inherited and be glad to have it.

My fuller morning ritual, maybe in the shower or seated in a quiet place intentionally, is something I call a *mantra stream*: in three hummed and prolonged syllables it goes, "grace and peace, all is well, I give thanks." I go up a half note on each middle syllable, like in a Hindu mantra.

Throughout the day, you can do this mantra, or one of your creation ("another day in paradise"), most anytime or anywhere, waiting for the dryer to stop, waiting for pages to finish copying, waiting at a stoplight, or riding either way on the commuter train. It could focus on the hallowedness around you and within you, most likely slowing down your heart rate through refreshing deep breaths.

At the end of the day, Lynda and I have adopted a ritual before bedtime. Each one of us names and reflects upon at least three special experiences of the day. Since then we have been more sure than ever that our daily lives are full and rich, and, therefore, life is a profound journey. After our time together, I do my own further reflections and close with this ritual, to myself: "I _____ (I fill in the appropriate adverb, e.g., "humbly" or "begrudgingly" – be honest) give thanks for the day I've had." Something simple and meaningful to you. Make up your own or borrow from this or some other source.

From morning till night, I suggest we give our day a theme through such rituals and tie the day together in one stream of self-consciousness awareness. *Thanksgiving* is as profound as anything I can think of. Under such a theme we can begin the day with thanksgiving for a new day, experience and reflect upon all the experiences of our day, and then at night slip into the awesome silence and darkness of creation as we breathe several sustained breaths that always come as sheer gift to be thankful for.

Experiencing our experience all day long, every day, for a lifetime, is what it's all about. I would dare to say there is no depth reality for us apart from our experience of depth reality, so wring the profound meaning out of every experience of every day of your life – and be thankful.

Verse 4

Oh that which is

Oh that which sees via my seeing
       . . . that tastes via my tasting
       . . . that touches via my touching
       . . . that hears via my hearing
Oh that which speaks via my speaking
       . . . that sings via my singing
       . . . that laughs via my laughing
       . . . that cries via my crying
Oh that which dreams via my dreaming
       . . . that creates via my creating
       . . . that prays via my praying
       . . . that rejoices via my rejoicing
Oh that which breathes via my breathing
       . . . that communes via my communing
       . . . that loves via my loving
       . . . that serves via my serving

Oh that which exists
       via the heart of my being
         is surely more
       via the heart of all being

~may 29, 2003

Reflection 5

Spirituality of Life

HUMANS HAVE BEEN GATHERING IN CIRCLES for at least 50,000 years, celebrating the good creation and telling stories about their depth encounters. We are a part of their ongoing circle because we too have stories about our depth experiences to share, which make us human.

Such experiences are triggered by our encounters in the realm of creation. As citizens of creation and as humans we can relate experiences we have of non-human nature, of social nature, of personal nature. (I will continue to talk about "nature" as not separate from but inclusive of humans.)

Let me tell you about one of my experiences with non-human nature. I am forever marked by the Blue Ridge Mountains in Virginia where I was born and raised. To this day, when they come into view from a distance, when I wind back up them, or when I fly by them, deep things happen in me. They are my native home. Recently I drove back to my mountains from the North Carolina piedmont and was enraged when I saw a mountain side ravaged by loggers. I railed and then I had to pull off the road to wipe away the tears. Each of us has stories of encounters with nature.

We all have stories of social encounters. Our family has lived in communities around the world, from a small Virginia town, to a ghetto on the West Side of Chicago, to a village in Indonesia called Kalapa Dua, to a village in India called Jawale. I can tell you stories through the night around a campfire of how encounters with the residents of those communities changed my life. Returning to Chicago recently, we visited the Fifth City community and walked through its preschool that our two sons attended many years before. It was awesome to see the dedication of the community teachers mold the young lives of the next generation of their African-American community.

We all have numberless personal stories, of joy and suffering, that we tell when the circle is right, stories about a dream we had or about a great longing. I have recounted in my memoir how I would climb the stairs as a boy, and when I got to the top I was breathless because of fear that something or someone would reach out and grab me from the dark room on the left as I reached for the light string. We all have our personal stories.

And we all have our religious or spirit stories about significant symbols for us, about what is deeply meaningful to us, or about our sense of calling. I could tell the story of how I got baptized twice or the story about the bullet that killed my President in 1963 and precipitated the biggest turning in my life.

Stories about our life encounters are the very stuff of our lives. That is one of the reasons we love art. Art tells stories about life experiences. I identify with the children in *To Kill a Mocking Bird* as they tell stories about Boo Radley and his haunted house. Similarly, I have shared in the experience of the last stanza of the song *The Rose*:

> Just remember in the winter
> Far beneath the bitter snows
> Lies the seed that with the sun's love
> In the spring becomes the rose.

To prove a point, will you please participate in an exercise? You don't have to write anything down unless you want to. Just read and think about your answer.

48

1. A memory of a deep experience for me in each of these categories:

   a. non-human nature _____
   b. social _____
   c. personal (joy)_____
   d. personal (suffering) _____
   e. religious/spirit _____
   f. art _____

2. My most profound experience (a-f) was _____
3. This experience was most about a) union, b) reverence, c) meaning, or d) _____
4. How this experience affected/changed me

   _____

5. I have had _____ deep experiences in my life:
   1-5
   5-10
   10-25
   25-50
   50-100
   100s
   1000s
6. This exercise has helped me to see that

   _____

So what's the point? Spirituality is about our everyday experiences, and sometimes in the midst of all these mundane experiences called life we come to know that we have been blessed by wonder-filled events, can-see-clearly-now events, open-my-heart events, sense-of-oneness events, reunion events, even life-changing events. Such events coming at us, breaking open our consciousness, make our life journeys profound. Such events build up memories that will grace us all our days.

Where do such events come from? They come from the center of life: something happens, we experience it, we may be awestruck, we tell stories about the experience, we interpret it, we recall it many times. Some such process indicates that we start with the life experience, not some belief system or doctrine handed down by a tradition. Our experiences of *spirit* happening in our lives are directly from the heart of life itself.

But a most basic belief or doctrine may take shape from my witness to a deep experience: I begin to declare that *spirit* is present in life and that *spirit* is at the center of life. We could then make word symbols such as *SEP* and *SATH* – a tiny tatoo on the hand would be nice – meaning "*spirit's* ever present" and "*spirit's* at the heart" of creation, as we have witnessed in our life experiences in the exercise above. This is the way of the spirituality of life, to witness to and report what has happened to us.

Spirituality is about our experiences of life. Each of us is therefore the high priest of the spirituality of life. As such, we bow to the heart of creation and say, "Life is very good the way it is."

Verse 5 *Christmas*

Why celebrate Christmas
Why such a hullabaloo
she asked Good question I said
But what answer will she listen to

Life is full of wonder
full of love and joy and peace
full of hope and communion
of possibility openness

You and I've experienced
such gifts many times and more
bringing meaning to our lives
filling full what seemed empty before

Remember all the times
in spite of doubt we could not
give into the lie of lies
that living is just a senseless plot

Life's what we celebrate
at Christmas the very ground
of meaning purpose and love
not despair and hopelessness abound

She said I've got it now
Ev'ry tiny baby's birth
regardless whose when or where
reveals the story of sacred worth

Yes life is so very good I said

~december 23, 2002

Reflection 6

spirit

LET ME BE AS CLEAR AS POSSIBLE: when I use the word "spirit," I am *not* talking about a God, a Designer, a First Mover, a Creator, a Super Consciousness, a Holy Spirit, a Great Spirit, a Self, or any name that could point to some supernatural something beyond the natural world.

At the same time, I intentionally use the word "*spirit*," yes, with a little "s" and italicized. Let me explain why and what I mean. First of all, there is a difference between *spirit* and the human spirit, with no italics. I have some control over my human spirit, but I have no control over *spirit*, which blows where it wills, as religious tradition reminds us. Second, since *spirit* is the most real thing in creation, it seems fitting to highlight it. (I'll forego italicizing nouns and pronouns that refer to *spirit*.)

Spirit is at the heart of all that has form or being. *Spirit* is a presence that was, is, and ever will be now. And *spirit* reveals the sacredness in everything in the universe. To my Hebrew fathers in the faith, the "Spirit of Yahweh" was closer to them than their breath. Building on their poetry, I say *spirit* is the inner breath of creation. *Spirit* is breath within breath, smile within smile, seeing within seeing, hearing within hearing. We appropriate *spirit* with our sixth sense, which operates within all our senses.

There is *spirit* beyond measure that fills full the universe and is forever present. Martin Buber has used the poetry of "the eternal Thou" (*I and Thou*, p. 92). Ken Wilber's best bit of poetry on the subject: "Spirit is always already present" (*The Eye of Spirit*, p. 281).

One of my favorite poets describes our encounter with *spirit* this way,

. . . here, in the other world, still terrestrial
myself, the same as before, yet unaccountably new.

. . . I put out my hand in the night, one night, and my hand
touched that which was verily not me,
verily it was not me. . . .

Ha, I was a blaze leaping up!
I was a tiger bursting into sunlight.
I was greedy, I was mad for the unknown.
I, new risen, resurrected, starved from the tomb,
starved from a life of devouring always myself,
now here was I, new-awakened, with my hand stretching out
and touching the unknown, the real unknown, the unknown
unknown. . . .

This is part of D. H. Lawrence's poem "New Heaven and Earth" (*The Complete Poems*, pp. 258-9). In it he articulates a meaning that is beyond pre-modern and modern thinking. Let me attempt an exegesis of key lines:

- He says "the other world, still terrestrial," meaning the other world is *in* this world. At his inspiration, I draw a diagram of the *other world in this world*:

THE
OTHER
WORLD . . .
IN THIS
WORLD

- This diagram appears simplistic but represents a shift in consciousness, even for us in our day who have been trying to express such thoughts for at least a generation. *Spirit* is not up there or out there, but in here (represented by the lines throughout the diagram), in this world. *Spirit's* where it's always been, and always will be, in this world, "still terrestrial." That's very good to know.
- Further, Lawrence says "verily not me, verily it was not me," meaning *spirit* is not me ("not I" for English teachers), not the universe, but only happens in the universe, in nature, which includes you and me.
- He calls *spirit* "the unknown, the real unknown, the unknown unknown." Aren't names fascinating?
- He says that *spirit* is all about *transformation*, making *what is* the "same as before, but unaccountably new."
- And I hear Lawrence saying – from his experience and from mine – that *spirit* is the most real thing in creation.

If all this is so, *seeing* and *relating* are the primal spiritual clues to the relationship between the universe and us. First of all, spirituality is about *seeing* something, being aware of something, realizing something. There is in creation, in all its events and elements, the revelation of grace – if we see through to what really is and accept its revelation. The process of seeing is what I have talked about in my other books as the *transparent event* or *transparency*, when we are given to see what is and are sometimes transformed, especially – second of all – when we self-consciously *relate* to what we see. We can choose, or not, to bow to the other we encounter, whether human or non-human.

Some would call this kind of talk *mystical*. I refrain from using that word if it infers there are some few who have spiritual experiences and that most don't. What I am talking about is an every-person experience of reality.

Banish spiritual elitism, where someone is further along the spiritual path, or some are closer to *spirit* than others. Impossible, for how can anyone or anything be any closer to *spirit* than anyone or anything else, that is if *spirit* is ever-present? From time to time, we all really see and are related with *spirit* through the other. Experiences of reunion are the ground of grace for every person because of the way *spirit* works in the universe, of which we all are full citizens and participants.

To reiterate, we all experience *spirit* because *spirit* happens in our relations with creation. Even though *spirit* is permeating every event and element of creation, it happens for us through our meeting with the other in creation. As Chuang Tzu (c.369-286 BCE) mythologizes,

> Can a man cling only to heaven
> And know nothing of earth?
> . . . To know one
> Is to know the other.
> To refuse one
> Is to refuse both.
> (*The Way of Chuang Tzu*, Thomas Merton, p. 88)

We know or experience *spirit* in our relations within creation: "to know one is to know the other." Conversely, "to refuse one is to refuse both," meaning "if we say we love God and hate the neighbor, we are liars" (the Christian *New Testament*). Jesus said, "the second is like the first: love of God and love of the neighbor." Or as Tillich says, "Everything can become a medium of revelation, a bearer of divine power. 'Everything' not only includes all things in nature and culture, in soul and history; it also includes principles, categories, essences, and values" (*Biblical Religion*, pp. 22-3).

Through our relationships in creation – either with wife, child, workmate, boss, schoolmate, enemy, salmon, water use, gas consumption, community relations, cultural or religious myths, politics, house and car purchase, etc. – we meet *spirit*, because *spirit* happens to us in our relationships with creation. If we *use* things or others, then we refuse *spirit*. If we wholeheartedly care for and honor the other, we very well might experience the power of *spirit* in that relationship, or experience the "eternal Thou." As Chuang Tzu says in the quote, heaven comes on earth through our deep relations of knowing.

So, *spirit* is not in some supernatural orbit beyond creation but happens quite naturally in and through our relations in creation. Sometimes in the *seeing* and *relating* we experience union, reunion, nirvana, blessedness, or heaven on earth – if only momentarily. Yet, each such moment inspires a profound memory and confirms the most real thing worth knowing, that *spirit's* presence is at the heart of creation.

Verse 6

Easter

Then she asked about Easter
the great Christian centerpiece
What about eternal life
I cannot make sense of that can you

      It is hard to explain I said
      that life is resurrection
      seeds shooting up from the earth
      butterfly winging from its prison

      about metamorphosing
      apartheid-ers forgiven
      Berlin walls tumble-ing down
      species from extinction's grave risen

      being born a second time
      new heart beating in my breast
      scales falling from my eyes
      blind but seeing life anew and yes

      miracles of reunion
      stirring ashes of our lives
      raising up the lame and dead
      by that power that's beyond our eyes

      by that power that gives us might
      gives us courage to overcome
      our despair and hopelessness
      new creatures of intercommunion

This is what we celebrate
during spring the awesome sound
of cracked cocoons rolling stones
and shouts of the forgiven resound

the splashing play of whales
future buzz of honey bees
sight for the blinded bigots
lasting peace among earth's enemies

Nonvisible and mysterious
power will surely raise the dead
will inspire our breath again
'tis the power of Easter I said

She said I think I've got it
ev'ry time I thought I'd died
the greatest secret of all
revealed to me life in death does hide

Yes life is so very good I said

~december 24, 2002

59

Reflection 7

that power

At the still point of the turning world. Neither flesh
    nor fleshless;
Neither from nor towards; at the still point, there the
    dance is. . . .
Except for the point, the still point,
There would be no dance, and there is only the dance.

~T.S. Eliot ("*Burnt Norton*," *Four Quartets*)

THE PREVIOUS REFLECTION, "*spirit,*" is what I'd call a secular-religious statement. This one is a more secular statement about *that power* at the heart of creation.

What we perceive as real is what we experience through the five senses and accompanying emotions. In the West, at least, we have been throwing out the concept of other-worldliness for hundreds of years as we have settled into living in our one world. But we have not been all that successful in finding fulfilling images and symbols that replace the ones we've thrown out.

In another day, there were those who described for us our interior castles and states of being that were maps for our profound journey. Today we are lucky if we have more than psychological guidelines gleaned from how-to literature and role-modeled on television. We have been called a shallow generation or told that we live in flatland, experiencing little height nor depth. When we attempt to interpret the meaning of events and encounters in our lives, we seem to grab for platitudes: just one day at a time; you can cope; life is short so live it up; what a thrill.

To help us deal with our underlying malaise and to point us toward fulfillment, let us consider deeper metaphors for our interior journey. Tillich's "the ground of meaning" intrigues me, as does this language by Brian Swimme, a physicist, from his book with the poetic title *The Hidden Heart of the Cosmos* (p. 104): "the Great Power . . . gave birth to the universe . . . and continues to be involved with giving birth in every interaction throughout the universe." Einstein wrote his friend Otto Juliusburger (1942), "we never cease to stand like curious children before the great Mystery into which we were born."

I believe there is a deep dialogue going on in the universe that is not the same as the dialogue going on between you and me, or between a mountain and me, or between an insect and me. We are all caught up in a dialogue that is not just the universe dialogue, but is the primal, interior dialogue with *that power* at the heart of the universe. It is what Ursula Goodenough, a cell biologist, refers to as dialogue with "the sacred depths of nature" – "nature" meaning to me everything in the universe, including us humans.

Below is my diagram of the key interior ways we humans relate to the givenness of our universe:

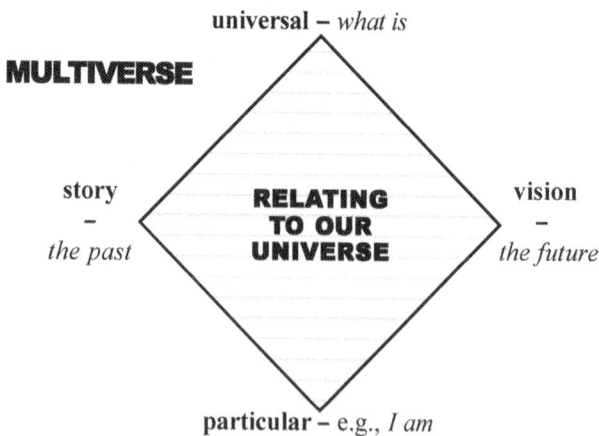

universal – *what is*

MULTIVERSE

story
–
the past

**RELATING
TO OUR
UNIVERSE**

vision
–
the future

particular – e.g., *I am*

There is something I call an *ever-present, all-pervasive power* in the universe (represented in the diagram by all the lines in the diamond) that presents me with the possibility to relate to *all that is*, to *any particular* (including self), to a *story* about where we came from, and to a *vision* about where we're going. The possibility of relation is real because I am left with the decision to have, or not to have, what actually is – through these four relational dimensions of our universe. The possibility given by *that power* never stops; it constantly calls for my *yea* or *nay* in all directions of space and time. Through such decisions to relate, I can experience profundity in my human life in this universe. My *yes* response to reality, as it encounters me, is the beginning of wisdom. Interior life quality, whether enlivening or debilitating, corresponds to the way we choose to relate to our given universe.

Some fundamental questions, which are really one question, come in our encounter with *that power* in our universe within the multiverse:

- How do we get over our pre-modern other-worldliness and our modern and post-modern worldliness, both of which are killing our human spirit and thereby killing the earth at our hands?
- How do we know that all is connected: universe and human, power and matter?
- How do we know that the *mysterious power* is ever-present in universe existence?
- How do we stay in touch with the interior reality of the external universe?
- Maybe the one question is How do we develop the sixth sense of *depth seeing* that is crucial to the survival of the earth community, including us humans?

"See or perish!" admonishes Teilhard de Chardin (*The Human Phenomenon,* p. 3): see that the universe before our very eyes is sacred instead of something to be used. He gives us clues to the interior dimension of reality in his writings: "matter is transparent . . . in relation to spirit"; "reality has become transparent"; there is a "mysterious presence shining in the depths of things"; at "the heart of matter"; at "the very heart of reality"; at the "depths of every event, every element" there is "a numinous presence" (*Hymn of the Universe*). Teilhard is describing the way creation is: there is *that power* at the heart of all that is; therefore, if we but see creation the way it is, sacred to the heart, transformation can follow.

There is an interior power in the universe:

Jack Nicholson: "What if this is as good as it gets?"
Louis Armstrong: "What a wonderful world."

Teilhard de Chardin: "See or perish!"
Julia Ward Howe: "Mine eyes have seen the glory. . . ."

What is our interior journey about? Putting the clues together, I say,

sometimes it happens that we really see the universe the way it is, mysteriously sacred to the core. We are changed and our universe is changed.

What I'm trying to describe is at least mysterious, not me, not even universe – while it is happening only in my universe. There is more than physical matter, which only makes up about 27 percent of the universe, and dark matter, which makes up the other 73 percent of the universe. There is 100 percent *mysterious power* that fills full our universe.

Those scientists who think they know the theory of

everything, whether it be relativity, quantum mechanics, or string theory – or the combination of all scientific theories – are deceived if they think they can have a theory of everything that does not take into account the *mysterious power* at the heart of everything. How very reduced!

I appreciate the poetry of Ken Wilber on the subject: "a Presence that has no within or without, the ultimate Mystery permeates the Kosmos with an Obviousness that is too simple to believe, too close to see, too present to be reached" ("WTC," Part III).

With such poets I declare that . . .

> the *nonvisible power* is more real than visible power, and all humans, if not all creation, experience *that power*;

> therefore, all of us are on a sacred, universal journey because of *that power* at the heart of all and us all;

> and *that power* is out to transform us, and creation through us, if we but see and respond.

Believing this, I bow to and give thanks for *that power* at the heart of creation.

Verse 7

*heart of creation**

from the heart of creation
whether it be
dinosaur or the latest e-

vent that invades consciousness
whether it be
a birth or catastrophe

spirit is happening
whether it be
now or then in eternity

~*october 2001*

---

* Adapted from my *Our Universal Spirit Journey: Reflection and Verse for Creation's Sake*, p.112.

Section Two

Communion

Spirit journey: the experience of **communion** with the power at the heart of creation that motivates us to be agents of intercommunion.

Reflection 8

Communion within Creation

In and through this [universe] community we enter into
communion with that numinous mystery.
  ~Thomas Berry ("Cosmology of Religions")

Awesome moments of communion with what is:

Suckling at my mother's breast as a babe . . .
  communion with my mother
Walking the trail in the moonlight . . .
  communion with mother nature
Hugging the one I would marry. . .
  communion with my mate
Looking down on my hometown from a plane . . .
  communion with environs
Being licked by Lulu, our dog, as I studied theology . . .
  communion with a another species
Receiving granddaughter's mercy during great pain . . .
  communion with next generations
Seeing my Blue Ridge Mountain after an absence . . .
  communion with my home
Staring into the eyes of a seagull at Caswell Beach . . .
  communion with a strange creature
Watching my grandson bend over to kiss a flower . . .
  communion with one in communion
Hearing Buddhist monks growl chants in Thai temple . . .
  communion with a enigmatic tradition
Climbing up in a 5000-year-old pyramid on the Nile . . .
  communion with my ancestors

Conversing with Udesh in a Indian village at midnight . . .
   communion with one of 6.4 billion local persons
Hearing Mama say "I love you, John" as she died . . .
   communion with utter mystery
Meditating on my breathing . . .
   communion with the breath within my breath

When communion happens
   sometimes I experience the other as a *thou*
   sometimes I experience the *eternal thou*
And when that happens I experience
   much more than neurological sensations
   as I am united with the other
   and embraced in the unity of being
Sometimes I believe again
   because trust is reborn during communion
   as I am held in being
   within all my communities

Some say time space matter and energy are all there is
   But these four are hardly the grand total of it all
   Over under and permeating them is
      the numinous mystery
         without which they are but so much stuff
         with which they are consecrated being

Great communion keeps us bowing to creation
keeps us saying I give thanks for your being
With hands pressed together at the heart
   people bow to greet each other with *namaste*
   meaning *spirit's* at the heart of creation
      at the heart of you
      experienced in communion

Communion happens in little and big ways:

Sing a simple love song and discover yourself
      singing to all that is
Gaze at a flickering candle and commune
      with light in darkness
Watch an ant colony and commune
      with a community in action
Read the *Psalms* and commune with David's Lord
Hold your new baby and commune in unspeakable joy
See bulldozers pushing Jewish bodies into mass graves
      and commune with millions dying of genocide
Hear the African Children's Choir
      and commune with millions dying of AIDS
Break bread and spill wine
      and commune with the goodness of life itself

Every piece of creation is blessed is sacred
For *spirit* is revealed through each
      to be communed with
Since every created thing has a heart

Communion is the "union with" all that is
SiddhArtha and Francis knew
      each *other* is sister brother father or mother
We experience union
      in communion
            with each and every one
            in creation

For in reality we are One
      and through *spirit's* power of *communion*
      we experience this fact of all facts

As Thomas says

> "In and through this universe community
> we enter into communion
> with that numinous mystery"

. . . at the heart of everything that is.

~february 17, 2003

An exuberant expression of the life of communion is found in Basil
Sharp's book, *The Adventure of Being Human.*

Verse 8 *Oh I Don't Know*

Two lonely leaves hanging from a limb
tossed in the early winter wind
considering the day of their fall
What will happen after we descend

Said one to the other: What if
when we land there is nothing more
nothing except we rot away
Wouldn't that be an awful shame

Said the other: Oh I don't know
From dust to dust is the promise
and I'm sort of fascinated
by the process of changing form

The first: Isn't *transformation*
a word for raving romantics
who believe in happy endings
We're about to experience death

Said the second: Oh I don't know
The way the word *death* comes to me
is something like what happened when
dinosaurs died in the 60s

and vegetation really thrived
That is the big picture on death
I guess it all makes sense to me
thinking of what comes after us

The first: Maybe the universe
and the earth will figure it out
All we have to do is be blown
And soon they did float to the ground

The second: That was sort of neat
an experience we've not had
First: Yea here we are yet alive
Is death only a metaphor

Oh I don't know said the second
I'm sort of enjoying the view
From down here it does give us a
new perspective on everything

Then asked the first: Do humans think
about what happens after death
Oh I don't know said the second
But they don't need to be afraid

Two lonely leaves hanging from a limb
tossed in the early winter wind
considering the day of their fall
What will happen after we descend

~december 14, 2002

Reflection 9

"Fil Lik Rolty"

THIS PAST YEAR OF TRANSITION has occasioned a vocational crisis for me. After selling our family business, relocating to Greensboro to be close to the grandchildren during their formative years, at least, I enjoyed a few months of retirement. But soon the truth came, "Lynda, what are you going to do now? You can't retire."

My teaching certificate had long expired. I easily fell into a temporary job with the federal court system. They wanted someone to type reports about persons being considered for pretrial supervision, as an alternative to incarceration. I greeted them when they came in for their weekly conferences, and I watched their children while they took their urine tests. I began to notice the pattern in their reports: failure in school. Something began to stir in me. Although the court asked to take the permanent position, I knew I was recalled to teaching.

Not wanting the long preparation hours that a regular teacher has, I applied to be an assistant. The opening was in the second grade where I was shared by three different classes. Getting to know eighty-five children and three different young teachers pushed me hard. I came home exhausted and was second-guessing my decision.

To complicate matters, I followed the classroom procedure for disciplining a student for a minor infraction, but failed to inform the classroom teacher. There I was, being reprimanded by a young teacher, who even said my style was "too nice." I was humiliated and was considering going back to the federal court job when the Thanksgiving bulletin board went up.

Pinned on it were the teachers' names on pumpkin envelopes to receive notes of thanks from students and other teachers. Much to my surprise, my envelope was stuffed. The note that really got to me came from the student least likely to succeed in class and in life. His circumstances and background put him in line to be one of those federal court cases. He was my special reminder of why I had decided to return to teaching. His note read,

Der Mis Cock,

You is the nicst techer. You mak me fil lik rolty.

Delrico

Reading that note, especially, was a transforming moment, wherein I experienced a new passion to give my gifts to my second graders. Delrico made *me* feel like royalty.

~lynda l. cock, 2001

<u>Verse 9</u> *Aussie Wisdom*

What must I know before I go?

What will I do if I have to?

What will I be if really me?

These are the questions they tell us

we must answer if we live in

the world of civilization.

But you know, matc,

they don't know their

head from their bum.

I think it is more a question

of seeing life's answer in the

mystery of communion.

~november 17, 2002

Reflection 10

Giving Thanks for the Fog

ONE SUMMER DAY LAST YEAR, Lynda and I got off the Great Smoky Mountain Highway and started driving the Blue Ridge Parkway between Balsam Mountain and Asheville. Several thousand feet up, we entered the fog and had to pull over and stop. We were scared to go farther, especially as we noticed, directly to our side, stretches of road without guardrails. We feared the terrifying drop.

A weird sensation it is to be enshrouded in fog on a mountain pass. You are going along and suddenly you cannot see the way. You experience helplessness and fear. You feel out of control.

This is the way of our life journey if we live long enough or self-consciously. Driving along with a sure sense of what we're doing, simply out to enjoy the trip, we experience being fogged in. Blinded. What used to make sense doesn't make sense all of a sudden, because we've lost vision and direction. Danger looms. We are stopped on an out-of-the-way road. We're trapped in a glaring darkness in the midst of fog. We experience dark in the middle of the day, in the middle of our journey.

Fear not. This is the way *spirit* works. Sometimes it blinds us, stops us, fills us with fear, all for the very good reason of explaining its truths. Sometimes it asks big questions: Where do you think you're going? And why?

Lynda and I took out our picnic basket and began to eat inside the car. After a while she began to talk about times in her journey and ours where we had been blinded and felt helpless and lost. I began to add to the conversation that went deeper and deeper. We were as awed by the conversation as we were by the fog.

Then we sat in silence and stillness. I said something like, "We spend about as much time in dark during our lives as we do in the light. We wouldn't be very lively during the day without the refreshment of the dark of the night, would we?"

Parked at the scenic overlook, where we could not see, sometimes we begin to see what is really there. We can hold hands, breathe deeply, share our deepest memories and feelings, and see with the inner eye. Sometimes we begin to give thanks for being blinded. Enfolded in the fog of life sometimes brings vision and deep communion with the universe and with *spirit's* journey.

We begin to understand the beauty in the art of oriental scenes of mountains enveloped by fog. For thousands of years, holy persons have been attracted to such places. Me too, now. I have since downloaded such a scene for my computer screen. It reminds me of *spirit's* way and I give thanks.

Verse 10

YAAAA from a Universe Shrink

The therapy of self-acceptance
is on the rise in self-centered cultures
leading to delusion the poor souls
that want to believe I can
if I will just accept myself

But you are not created that way
What you can do is accept the other
outside the boundary of your skin
be they human or non-human
be she the universe herself

The fact is you are accepted
by her who is not yourself
You just show up in the flow
of this universe on the move
from creation to creation

That's really quite enough
don't you think when you think
You are at just this moment
sublimely nestled in the flow
of the cosmic oneness

But you don't feel accepted
Who said you were supposed to
Since you are now in the flow
be that the meaning of your life
a part of the ongoing goingonness

One more time let me say
she accepts just who you are
Just try to get off the earth
Try to get out of the universe
Your acceptance is complete

So please get it straight
Look up from your navel
and live the way the rest
of creation is living
like trees cows and neutrinos

Get on with your life
Look up and out and live
because you are accepted
by all that was and is and will be
even though you don't feel like it

If you still yearn for acceptance
let me say it one last time
YOU ARE ALWAYS ALREADY ACCEPTED
YAAAA That's all you need to know
Your self-acceptance obsession be gone

That will be $400 please

~december 11, 2002

Reflection 11

It Takes a Universe

THE APARTMENT where we have lived for the past two years has recently come under new ownership and has a new name: Woodland Park Apartments, replacing the more elitist sounding Regency Apartments. Here we have enjoyed a natural setting in an urban city.

In the fall when the undergrowth had died back, five-year-old granddaughter Kaitlyn and I explored the woods behind our place and discovered a little creek (probably created by the runoff from the huge amount of asphalt in our parking lot) where we could "fish" and look for little creatures. John and Jeremiah helped us create a step over a marshy place. We collected various kinds of nuts and seed pods that had fallen from the trees and pretended that they were our food.

We've been trying to expose the grandchildren to all the wonders around us in this setting, the bugs under rocks, crawdads in the water, different kinds of leaves and seeds and how they develop over the seasons, oohing and aah-ing over the beauty of a lunar moth attached to our doorway instead of screaming at its "otherness," teaching them to respect all creation, and we have read them books about the glory of the universe about us.

Little Nolan, who is three, surprised us the other day as he came into the apartment and saw a blooming plant. He stopped and talked to the plant, "Hello, you beautiful flower. You are so pretty, I want to kiss you." Then he bent over and did just that. We have been amazed at the way our little ones respond to creation.

Thomas Berry, our universe mentor here in Greensboro, goes beyond the well-known African proverb "it takes a village to raise a child" and says

> It takes a universe
> to make a child both
> in outer form and inner
> spirit. It takes
> a universe to educate
> a child. A universe
> to fulfill a child.

> Each generation presides over the meeting of these two.
> (on bookmarks he gave out after November 1999)

Thomas talks about the need to teach children to read the wonder and creativity of the universe even before we teach them to read from books.

This summer, I have received new motivation for my role as grandparent and as a second grade teacher: to introduce children to the universe in which they live and move and have their being.

I tell you, I love this revolutionary job!

~lynda l. cock, june 28, 2001

RICH IS NOT

HOW MUCH YOU HAVE
OR WHO YOU ARE.

RICH IS

COMMUNING WITH
THE HEART OF CREATION.

Reflection 12

Life Is Full of Surprises

VERY EARLY THIS MORNING I was reading my e-mails. There was one from Julie in Australia saying the books had come so quickly and in great shape. I said, "Yes!" as I gave a small Tiger Woods arm pump. On to the next one from Beret in Minnesota: "John, the book was delivered oil-soaked and is coming apart." That stopped my celebration.

Immediately the TV scene replayed itself: the postal workers were picking up the strewn mail from the wrecked mail truck that had left Greensboro on I-40. A bad rain storm. The driver was killed. And my day's work of packaging my new books was probably on that truck going west. How's all that for a connected universe?

I woke up Lynda and we began spinning about the driver's family and what other "important mail" was on that truck – quite a tangent. From there we spun out thinking about all the life-stopping surprises that come to each of us: a routine doctor's exam that reveals cancer, or a brain aneurysm, or a clogged artery or two. Or what about a divorce announcement from a son you've raised.

We were feeling just a little angst as we rehearsed that life too often comes as sheer, out-of-our-control, overwhelming mystery – which is not what we call it when it happens.

Then, before we could cap our awesome conversation, there followed an eruption of questions from wherever: Why me? What next? Why is life like this? Can I deal with it? What does "All is possible!" mean in these situations? Where is *spirit* in all this?

I am amazed that I just read a couple of e-mails and had a conversation with myself, Lynda, and *spirit* – that wants to make sure through such surprises that I don't forget that it is always already present. My day is reaching transforming proportions already and I'm still in my pajamas.

I'm left with the full knowledge that I am journeyed, that I am hardly the captain of my fate, and that daily I have multiple opportunities to say "yea" or "nay" to life's surprises. Somehow, this reflection has enabled me to say "yes" to this awesome day so far.

I find a little comfort in realizing that multi-zillion galaxies don't even know what has already happened to me today, and ole man river just keeps on rolling along. What a wonderful world.

Exercise 12

Experiences of Communion

A. Return to the listing of awesome events on pages 19-23, "Have You Experienced the Mystery?" Read over your written experiences and put a "c" in the outer margin beside each one wherein you experienced communion.

B. Then write down at least five general types of circumstances or situations when communion sometimes happens to us humans, for example, *when I am awed by the power of nature*:

1.

2.

3.

4.

5.

C. Write an overall reflection about communion:

Verse 13

Amazing Grace

Amazing grace, ten thousand times,
has touched the heart of me;
I once was lost but now am found,
was blind but now I see.

Through mighty, awesome turns in life
I have already come;
'tis grace that makes me whole through faith,
and grace will lead me on.

Amazingly, since primal star,
grace joined this voice of mine
with all creation near and far
to celebrate sublime.

When we've been journeyed all our days
by grace till breath is gone,
we'll no less yearn to sing its praise
than when we'd first begun.

~original by John Newton, 1779;
revised october 7, 2002

Reflection 13

Soul Satisfaction

I WAS READING about another's spirit journey before turning off the light. Later, about 3 a.m., I woke up from a dream. It was a vision of spirituality for humanity:

> Masses of humans are walking the Earth in search of a fulfilled life. They have given up on political, economic, and cultural promises.
>
> At the first stop they participate in universally religious rituals. They rehearse them diligently for months but then walk on, for the rituals appealed primarily to aesthetics and their personal salvation. Their souls were not deeply satisfied.
>
> At the second stop they hear a learned man articulate a set of well-formulated beliefs. They listen to them diligently and study and discuss them for months but then walk on, for the beliefs appealed primarily to the development of their minds and morals. Their souls were not deeply satisfied.
>
> At the third stop they participate in multiple missions. They engage in them diligently for months but then walk on, for the missions appealed primarily to their sense of duty and responsibility. Their souls were not deeply satisfied.
>
> At the fourth stop they listen to a youth talk about the presence at the heart of creation that enfolds them. She tells them, "Commune with that presence and you will find life." The masses stayed on for a lifetime. Their souls were deeply satisfied.

I sat up in bed with a start and began pondering the meaning of my dream. In light of deeply *unsatisfied* souls, one big question remains: What is the key to soul satisfying journeys for humans? This question will not go away because I sense it has to do with our destiny.

Of late, three statements, one ancient and two contemporary, begin to answer this big question and therefore give me hope:

> Jesus talked about *spirit* within, without, and always at hand (JPC, *The Transparent Event*, p. 165).

> [I]n spirit . . . nature is timelessly enveloped. . . . Spirit in its human manifestation is a response of man to . . . *Thou* . . . which appears and addresses him out of the mystery. . . . (Martin Buber, *I and Thou*, pp. 24; 39).

> Somehow, no matter what your state, you are immersed fully in everything you need for perfect enlightenment. . . . One hundred percent of Spirit is in your perception right now. . . . [T]he trick . . . is to recognize this ever-present state of affairs, and not to engineer a future state in which Spirit will announce itself. . . . Spirit is the only thing that has never been absent (Ken Wilber, *The Eye of Spirit*, pp. 281; 296).

Here are clues to the big question: *spirit* or Spirit – or whatever we wish to call it – is always here and now; we humans commune with this present reality; communing with it is an everyday experience and is an every-person experience. In sum, these clues communicate that we humans can find soul satisfaction in this life, in this creation, just as we are, here and now.

For most of us, however, communing with *spirit's presence* does not come naturally after we leave childhood. We seem to live mostly in our personal worlds, and normally we do not consciously commune with *spirit*. Yet, as the three statements above say, *spirit* is the intimate presence of our lives. As Buber says, we are in *spirit's envelope*, like fish swimming in water and creatures of earth surrounded by air. But like fish and all creatures, we mostly fail to recognize that which embraces us. Nonetheless, *spirit* is always present.

Communing with *spirit* is the key to humanity's journey. That's what the Buddha, Abraham, Jesus, and Mohammed knew in their hearts and what they came to declare and show.

This is what Brother Lawrence knew and why people came from all over to sit in his monastery kitchen with him to learn about *practicing the presence*, as he called it. He would have me commune with *spirit's presence* right here in the kitchen as I wash the dishes; right here in the study as I write this book; right here in the bathroom as I shower; right here in the dining room as I eat and dialogue with Lynda; right here in front of the doctor as he checks me for glaucoma; right here on the golf course as I walk down the fairways with our two sons; right here in the hospital as I talk with a dying friend; right here in the park as I play with our two grandchildren; right here on our tree-lined route as we walk together.

As the youth in the dream said, "Commune with that presence and you will find life." As we commune with and practice the presence of *spirit*, we begin to experience soul satisfaction and begin to see and relate to all others as *thou*.

(Please write your reflections on the next page.)

My Reflections

1. What words and phrases caught my attention? (I go back and mark them, if I haven't already.)

2. I recall my responses while reading this Reflection.

3. I recall my past searches for *deep satisfaction*, using descriptive phrases for such attempts (e.g., the romantic search).

   a.

   b.

   c.

   d.

4. I mark the words mentioned in the three quotes – e.g., *spirit, Thou, or Spirit* – and later in the Reflection that resonate most with me; or I choose other words.

5. What do I need in order to commune with *spirit's presence*?

6. *Deep satisfaction of the soul* is possible for me, *yes* or *no*?

7. How will I know when I have experienced *soul satisfaction*?

8. The key to spirituality for humanity is . . .

M14 *Communion Meditation*

From the previous Reflection, "Soul Satisfaction," pick one of the following phrases that attracts you:

> *spirit is at hand*
> *I and thou*
> *spirit's present*
> *here and now*

Get comfortable, close your eyes, and several times, as you take deep breaths, tighten your body muscles and release them. Do this till you feel relaxed.

Start to repeat the chosen phrase to yourself aloud if you are alone, or silently if you are in a group, moving your lips. Repeat the phrase slowly for at least ten minutes.

You will have many thoughts, feelings, and diversions. Simply acknowledge them by name. For example, if you start thinking about a person, name that person and refocus on repeating the phrase; if you start to cry, say to yourself, "I am crying," and refocus on repeating the phrase. If you hear a sound, say to yourself, "I heard thunder," and refocus on repeating the phrase.

At the end of the chosen time, stand up, with eyes open and with your hands together touching your heart, bow in four directions, saying or moving your lips, "I bow to thee."

After your practice, write out your diversions, your feelings, your experience of the experience, and a souvenir from the meditation to take with you. Then, on the next page, write a paragraph on "Communion Is."

Section Three

Intercommunion

Spirit journey: the experience of communion with the power at the heart of creation that motivates us to be **agents of intercommunion**.

Verse 15

Love All of Nature

The universe is a swirl of nature,
as the stars and sea and jungle adhere.

There are other parts of this cosmic world:
we humans were into nature hurled.

A tad less than angels we humans are:
homo sapiens as good as a star.

Ev'ry bit a part of the universe,
and not one thing is in any way worse.

20k orangutan kin remain,
begging us not to take their kind in vain.

During extinctions there must surely come
from the heart of us humans more freedom

To care for all *a tad less than angels'*,
delighting in them, reversing farewells.

Is it not our natural role to care
if keener awareness we humbly bear?

Mothers love most the child in greatest need
because nature's way is not guaranteed.

Center of all until Copernicus,
humans' show no longer, except to bless.

Toynbee's line and Dietrich's prison quote,
world thus come of age will hardly connote

We humans have not come of age for sure
and won't until we love all of nature.

~january 3, 2002

A profound example of the interdependence of all of nature is in the meditation of "Interbeing," *The Heart of Understanding*, by Thich Nhat Hanh.

Reflection 14

Intercommunion

"INTERCOMMUNION" IS A WORD THOMAS BERRY USES throughout his works. I asked Thomas the other night where he got the word. He assured me he borrowed it from someone, but could not recall anyone in particular.

With the word "intercommunion" I am not writing about the sacrament of Holy Communion among different Christian denominations. They write about the conditions for sharing the elements of wine and bread or withholding the same from other Christian groups as they guard against "indiscriminate intercommunion" – a most provocative phrase.

"Intercommunion," as I use the word here, is about our relationship with the universe, with planet earth, with all species, with humans near and far, from our family to our so-called enemies. Intercommunion is the way life is for creation, an intercommunion of subjects, not a collection of objects, again to borrow from Thomas.

To get a sense after "intercommunion," I offer two lists: *first*, intercommunion is about what essentially belongs together:

Intercommunion is Born out of Communion with Creation

Intercommunion . . .
    . . . *is the way life is, what essentially is*
    . . . *is the fundamental fact of our oneness as creation*
    . . . *is interconnectedness and interdependence*
    . . . *is born out of an experience of communion*
    . . . *is a universe-community-individual subject affair*

Second, "intercommunion" is about our participation with what is:

Intercommunion is Conscious Participation with Creation

Intercommunion . . .
. . . *is a covenantal **Yes** to creation*
. . . *is an I-thou, not an I-it, relationship with what is*
. . . *is a demonstration of unity, soul to soul*
. . . *is lived out in authentic community*
. . . *is an expression of deep care and love for creation*
. . . *is manifest in local and universal sacrificial service*
. . . *is the lifestyle of reconciliation*

I will primarily go with this second understanding of "intercommunion," assuming the first. I will mean that our experiences of communion motivate us toward reconciling acts of intercommunion. Therefore, to sum up the threefold rationale of this book:

> At one with the *heart of creation*
> – with the power of *spirit* –
> we experience *communion* . . .
> that motivates us toward *intercommunion.*

Spirit connects me with the rest of creation in my search for community. When I experience this, I grasp why I'm here: *to be family to creation,* which is *intercommunion.*

Is this hard to imagine for any of us? Not really, for we all in so many ways are family to creation. We are naturally family to our families. We are family to our circle of friends. We are family to our team at school, at work, in our volunteer organizations. We are family to our animals and gardens inside and outside our living quarters. We are family to the land on which we live.

We also understand, at times, that we are family with creation: with the sun that is indispensable to nourishment,

102

to the water we drink, to the harvest from the soil and other creatures that we eat for food, to the air that we breathe. And to services of untold numbers of fellow humans. We are part of the big family of creation, without whom we could not live. Similarly, there are many that depend on us for survival. This becomes more evident each day as the decisions we make influence our greater family of ecosystems, e.g., through global warming.

We see that "family" does not just apply to our relationships with humans but also with our relationships with the rest of creation. Brother and sister humanity and mother earth are our family, whether we think so or not, whether we like it or not. As family is the quality of intercommunion, likewise, family is who we intercommune with, whether soulfully or not.

This brings us to the crux of intercommunion: we've got family, period. How do we relate to the family we've got? As always, we relate well, not so well, and poorly. That's why intercommunion at its core is about *reconciliation*: how we go about asking forgiveness and treating the family as it should be treated, with deep respect and justice for all – treating them as family.

With this profound, yet simple, metaphor of family, I am talking about our experience, vision, ethics, and vocation of intercommunion.

Our Experience of Communion/Intercommunion

> When we experience consciousness of the unity in which we are embedded, the sacred whole that is in and around us, we exist in a state of grace. At such moments our consciousness perceives not only our individual self, but also our larger self, the self of the cosmos. The gestalt of unitive existence becomes palpable.
> **~Charlene Spretnak** (*States of Grace*, p. 24)

103

Our Vision of Intercommunion

[Communion as] participation guarantees the unity of a disrupted world and makes a universal system of relations possible. **~Paul Tillich** (*ST* I, p. 177)

Community cannot feed for long on itself. It can only flourish where always the boundaries are giving way to the coming of others from beyond them, unknown and undiscovered brothers and sisters. **~Howard Thurman** (*Creation Spirituality* magazine, Spring '97)

Our Ethics of Intercommunion

By responding to a crisis in God's creation, we're coming closer to God's law and God's love. [My words would be, "we're intercommuning."] ("Making Spiritual Connections," conversation with **Paul Gorman**, *The Environmental Magazine*, Nov/Dec 2002, Vol. XIII, No. 6, p. 9).

The fundamental fact of human awareness is this: "I am life that wants to live in the midst of other life that wants to live." A thinking man feels compelled to approach all life with the same reverence he has for his own. Thus, all life becomes part of his own experience. From such a point of view, "good" means to maintain life, to further life, to bring developing life to its highest value. "Evil" means to destroy life, to hurt life, to keep life from developing. This, then, is the rational, universal, and basic principle of ethics. ("**Albert Schweitzer** Speaks Out," 1964).

Our Vocation of Intercommunion

The main human task of the immediate future is to assist in activating the *intercommunion* of all the living

and nonliving components of the earth community.
~Thomas Berry (Principle 12, *Thomas Berry and the New Cosmology*, p. 108)

All our human affairs – all professions, occupations, and activities – have their meaning precisely insofar as they enhance this emerging world of subjective *intercommunion* within the total range of reality.
~Thomas Berry (*The Dream of the Earth*, p. 136)

Intercommunion is the circumference, height, and depth of our relationships in creation. Intercommunion is the fact *prior to* and the *context for* our human ethical participation. Intercommunion is the care of all by all. And *spirit* at the heart of creation is that which motivates intercommunion within creation. Therefore, let us act from the heart.

Verse 16

Just *Yes* or *No*

I share the genes of a banana I found out
on *NOVA* tonight and felt connected
in a new way to all of life.

Found out we humans are 99 point 9 percent
the same gene-wise and I felt connected
in new ways to the 6 billion.

I did not find out tonight how we humans
really do differ from the animals
or from the other forms of life.

I think it has something to do with the way we
perceive truth, how we respond, how we choose,
and what are our basic values.

It is much more than species, nation, religion,
education, relative wealth, power –
we humans decide *Yes* or *No*.

Does that make us better than all the non-humans,
more evolved than rocks, worms, and waterfalls,
more conscious than bacteria?

With the 6 billion there's hardly a difference,
only color and a few other things,
not enough to shake a stick at.

The *Yes* and *No* don't seem to be any big deal
till we consider the human venture
and impact on the earth venture.

~october 2002

Reflection 15

Soulful Transformation

AT LUNCH TODAY with Thomas Berry we agreed we both are engaged in addressing the contradiction of our time, a seeming *soullessness* which has happened to us humans as a result of the technological age. Thomas said he was coming at this historically and culturally and that I was coming at it spiritually, and that we both were dedicated to the transformation of the human soul for the sake of restoring the planetary community, or what Martin Buber calls "a living mutuality."

We both appreciate Buber's *I and Thou* language because we find it talking about crucial transformation and in a way that honors and yet transcends religious traditions. Buber worked out for himself what it means to be in relationship with what he calls the eternal within the temporal. Though he was steeped in Jewish theology, he transcended it. He writes about what every person knows, that living is about reverence and bowing to what is. He stresses fully living our everyday lives, not Sunday lives. He understood, as we do, that humans and other elements of creation want to be honored as a *thou* and not used as an *it*. This is the fundamental sensibility with which we're born, something we don't have to learn. On this simple and profound premise, Buber did his universal, secular-religious brooding and writing.

I have gone through Buber's book *I and Thou*, first written in 1923, for the umpteenth time, and picked out those statements that hold the crux of his thought:

[I]n spirit . . . nature is timelessly enveloped. . . . Spirit in its human manifestation is a response of man to . . . *Thou* . . . which appears and addresses him out of the mystery. . . . Spirit is not in the *I*, but between *I* and *Thou* [*spirit* is manifest to us in the relation]. . . . Only in [our] power to enter into relation [with nature/humanity are we] able to live in the spirit. . . . Every particular *Thou* is a glimpse through to the eternal *Thou*. . . . [S]pirit can penetrate and transform the world of *It* (*I and Thou*, pp. 24; 39; 75; 100).

Buber is talking about our relation to *spirit* at the heart of creation. Instead of using *I-Thou* and *I-It* over and over, I have chosen "soul" and "soulless," knowing "soul" words have many meanings. He is saying to me that *spirit* can transform our *soullessness* (our seeing every particular of creation as an *it*) to *soulfulness* (our seeing every particular of creation as a *thou*). In our *thou* response to meeting *spirit* in every encounter, we begin to live soulfully, in the *spirit*, as a part of the soulful transformation of our age.

When we begin to ground Buber's understanding of reality, we experience its revolutionary possibilities. Out of the encounter with the ever-present *spirit* comes the awareness of *thou*, which brings to us the possibility to decide to treat the other as a *thou*. Therefore, what would a lifestyle of *soulfulness* look like in our relationships in the family, school, neighborhood, workplace, bioregion, nation, and globe?

As a member of a *family*, treating another member as a *thou* instead of an *it* would look like this: I would look at the other member eye-to-eye and listen from the heart, I would be the first to ask forgiveness and to forgive, I would hug and kiss members of the family a lot more, and I would help create symbols and rituals to remind us to stand present to the gracious moment-by-moment choice of treating another member as a *thou* and not an *it*.

As a participant in school, treating another member as a *thou* instead of an *it* would look like this: I would propose teaching basic skills of honoring all others, be they human or non-human.

As a neighbor in my neighborhood, treating another member as a *thou* instead of an *it* would look like this: I would get to know my neighbors and call them by name, I would create opportunities for the neighbors to get together and celebrate, I would help the neighborhood to comprehensively care for its human and non-human constituents.

As a worker in the workplace, treating others as a *thou* instead of an *it* would look like this: I would propose that all employees be given ownership and help to see that all have liveable wages and benefits.

As a citizen of the Piedmont bioregion, treating all citizens – not just humans – as a *thou* instead of an *it* would look like this: I would help us humans to realize that our bioregion is a sacred trust that sustains all.

As a national citizen, treating other citizens as a *thou* instead of an *it* would look like this: I would help others to glory in our non-human and human diversity, I would advocate that creation become the context for the rights of all.

As a planetary citizen, treating other citizens as a *thou* instead of an *it* would look like this: I would call attention to the places of greatest innocent suffering, especially among the earth's biosphere and the 85% of the humans who have less than livable conditions.

IN ALL OF THESE "I would's," I wish to catalyze *I-thou* relationships in every possible encounter with the particulars of creation, as Buber says, and as such be a self-conscious part of soulful transformation in our time. I wish to convert people not to a religious persuasion but to a reverent relationship with the constituent parts of creation, remembering that *spirit* meets us in the separation between *I* and *it* and calls forth our soulful response to treat others as *thou*. And sometimes in being a part of a transforming *I-thou* relation, we experience relation with the *eternal thou*, with *spirit* – but always through our relation with creation.

Is this a personal salvation approach? No. It is a universal transformation approach, knowing all things and all creatures are embraced and journeyed by the *spirit* at the heart of creation? Yes.

> Only in [our] power to enter into relation [with nature/ humanity are we] able to live in the spirit. . . . Every particular *Thou* is a glimpse through to the eternal *Thou*.

Make your own list of "I would's" and be sure that your life is absolutely full of possibilities for soulful living. Living in the *I-thou* relation, in the *spirit,* is what our lives are all about.

E17 *Thou Exercise*

For me, treating others as a *thou* instead of an *it* would
look like this . . .

. . . in my *family*, I would:
1.
2.
3.
. . . in my *school*, I would:
1.
2.
3.
. . . in my *neighborhood*, I would:
1.
2.
3.
. . . in my *bioregion*, I would:
1.
2.
3.
. . . in my *nation*, I would:
1.
2.
3.
. . . on my *planet*, I would:
1.
2.
3.
My reflection on all this:

Reflection 16

Agents of Intercommunion

JUST A FEW REMINDERS OF ATROCITIES in the 20th century: Hitler's Germany, 1940s, over 6 million Jews killed by the Nazis; genocide in Bosnia-Herzegovina, 1992-95; genocide in Rwanda, 1994 – in 100 days approximately 800,000 Tutsis and moderate Hutu politicians killed and 2 million refugees forced from their homes; Pol Pot's Cambodia, 1970s, 1.7 million people died in the "killing fields" at the hands of the Khmer Rouge; Stalin's Russia, no one knows how many millions were killed in purges, forced famines, and gulags.

Yet, was there not evil done in the name of race, creed, class, and gender in most every nation? How many Aborigines or Native Americans were pushed off their land, put on the dole or welfare, and died of alcoholism in Australia and North America? How many millions of Muslims and Hindus died in religious clashes in India during the century? How many millions lost all they had, if they were not killed, in Idi Amin's Uganda?

Already, in the 21st century, what about the evil of nineteen Muslim fanatics flying planes into the Twin Towers, the Pentagon, and almost into the White House, believing the USA is evil? In Israel, what about a suicide bomber who pulls a cord and blows himself up along with nineteen more on the bus – mostly children? Or when a terrorist with a shoulder missile downs a full airplane?

What can we do? Keep upping defense budgets? There is not enough money in the world to buy enough military might to deal with such evil and terror growing out of such hatred. Ask the Russians about the war in Afghanistan.

Ask the USA about the war in Vietnam. And the war in Iraq is not going very well either.

But this reflection is just for you and me, about what we can do about our day-to-day divisive ways. Are we still using abusive words such as "Jap," "commie," "nigger," "queer," "redneck," "wetback"? Or are our epithets less divisive – we think – like "right-winger," "liberal," "fundamentalist," "godless"?

I have been in a serious dialogue over the last few years with a friend I've known since he was a youth and I was ten years his senior. We can really get together on the likes of Bonhoeffer's life and works, but we have stumbled into big divides in our dialogue on subjects ranging from the environment to politics. We have even closed down the dialogue several times but keep reaching out to each other to open it back up.

Recently, after we were more divisive than usual over an article from the *New York Times*, a paper he strongly dislikes, he wrote me a long e-mail attachment laying out his position and his take on mine. I heard him in a new way through his rant. I responded and e-mailed a couple of lists:

Agents of Division (I hear us saying)

NYTimes
Fox News
Bill Moyers
Rush Limbaugh
political parties

Agents of Intercommunion (I am saying)

SiddhArtha Gautama
Jesus
Dalai Lama

Gandhi
Bonhoeffer
Bishop Tutu
Mandela
MLK, Jr.
Hammarskjöld
John Woolman
Mother Teresa
Thomas Berry
Lynda (my wife)

We shared grades, *A* to *F*, for the lists. That helped soften us up. I told him I was writing a book about "agents of intercommunion" and that our dialogue was a case in point. I thanked him for helping me to repent a little. I said *spirit* unites, sin divides. He understands such language and understands what I mean, especially since he has read all my books. He even bought multiple copies of a couple of them to give to friends and to teach in his adult Sunday School class.

In one e-mail I said, "God knows we have to stop reckless divisiveness. That is what Jesus would be doing today." He e-mailed back for us to "keep the dialogue going and let's drop the labels." And he included the words from a song sung by Del McCoury he likes (later he sent me the whole CD entitled "Del and the Boys"):

Recovering Pharisee (lyrics by Buddy Green)

> I'm a Pharisee in recovery.
> With new eyes I can see
> A big sinner in me.
> It's the way of my human heart
> To confess other people's sins,
> Reluctant to admit my part,
> Or the deeper problem within. . . .

115

These are times of divisiveness. Lance Marrow, the author of *Evil*, was on *NPR* radio the other day saying that there was the "good war," but in the 60s we began to talk about the "bad war" of Vietnam, started saying to each other as Americans that we are part of the evil in the world, which some Muslims were already saying. We then began to say Muslims are evil. "Now," he said, "it's gone crazy."

It doesn't seem to me that religious groups, the national elected leadership, the political parties, the media, Hollywood, or TV are doing major strategies to unite us. So, guess what. If it's going to be done, we'd better become agents of intercommunion every way we can in every encounter we can. Let's drop the labels and begin to go soul to soul.

All I've said thus far in this reflection is on the personal and social side. What about our sin against the rest of nature. During the last two hundred years, have we ever become abusive and divisive with Mother Earth and her/ our atmosphere!

We have a lot of repenting to do on this planet as we fashion new responses as agents of intercommunion. I was thinking about putting a one-page ad in the local paper or going on the community TV channel to invite people of all cultures, faiths, classes, persuasions to. . . . Help me out here.

(What would you, the reader, an agent of intercommunion, do to repent?)

Reflection 17

Divisive Words*

> The religious, moral and spiritual breakdown of our
> time has to do with religion and not with spirituality.
> **~Diarmuid Ó Murchú** (*Reclaiming Spirituality*, p. viii)

IN THE 21st CENTURY I am shocked when I pick up
my former hometown newspaper and read that a local
preacher is saying on the far-reaching local radio station
that the Roman Catholic Church is evil; that the Pope is
the anti-Christ; and that 60 percent of all Roman Catholic
priests have AIDS. A local clergy took the radio preacher
to task in the local newspaper and received a flurry of
phone calls at his home supporting the radio preacher's
beliefs, with such comments as

- "Why are you standing up for them [the Roman
  Catholics]?"
- "We're Holiness people out here, not Catholics," said
  one female caller before abruptly hanging up.
- "He said it, and he's a man of God."
- When asked, one caller said she got some of her facts
  about the Church of Rome from the *National Enquirer*.
- "There are a lot of people around here who agree
  with him."

Is it any wonder that religious wars are going on today
around the world, in spite of the Pope's recent confessions
of the sins of the Roman Catholic Church through the ages
and his plea for forgiveness; or in spite of the Lutheran
and Roman Catholic formal reconciliation pact in 1999,

117

500 years after the Reformation?

How do Christians begin to get along and come together, much less 6,400,000,000 human citizens of the globe? As the radio preacher proved, it is easy to divide people. We all know how hard the reverse is. Does the preacher not know that his calling is to bring people together so that we begin to celebrate our unity in the name of the ever-present *spirit*?

As an act of reconciliation, the radio preacher could begin by confessing his sins against Roman Catholics, the Pope, the priests, and the rest of the Christian church not like him, and beg for forgiveness. Why would that not be the Christian thing to do? Why would that not be following the admonition of his Holy Bible out of which he preaches and hears the holy command to repent face to face?

Maybe he could take one of his thirty-minute radio programs to beg for forgiveness publicly. And then, maybe, for extra penance, he could preach out of the five chapters of the *First Letter of John* for at least five weeks until he begins to believe that "If we say we love God, but hate others, we are liars. . . . The truth that Christ has given us is this: whoever loves God loves others also."

If reconciliation does not begin in the hearts of those who understand they are called to be their God's special instruments, then divisiveness will abound on earth, at war with "Thy kingdom come."

But it doesn't have to be this way. There is a power stronger than hate and war, the power at the heart of religion and life. Paul Tillich articulates *First John* radically:

It is a rare gift to meet a human being in whom love – and this means God – is so overwhelmingly manifest. . . . It is the presence of God Himself. For God is love. And in every moment of genuine love we are dwelling in God and God in us. (*The New Being*, p. 29)

118

My Reflections

1. I list examples of religious hate globally.

2. I have seen religious hate manifest itself locally in . . .

3. I list how I harbor religious hate (e.g., I stereotype radio preachers) . . .

4. What keeps religious hatred alive in us all?

5. Where have I recently seen repentance for religious hatred?

6. How can I repent of my religious hate?

7. How can I overpower hate with love, whether I'm religious or not?

---

*This reflection was adapted from my book *Motivation for the Great Work: Forty Meaty Meditations for the Secular-religious*, pp. 79- 81.

Verse 18

What gets me down

What gets me down these days is
our pattern of consumption
our use of the earth
our abuse of the ozone
our denial of destroying the ecosystems

war
poverty
wealth
HIV/AIDS
addiction
population
hate

But as Søren says
authentic despair
has within it the cure –
possibility and necessity –
the power of conversion
which is grounded in *spirit*

To think we are going
to deal with all this
without radical conversion of
      spirit
      values
      priorities
      actions
is the biggest illusion

Let despair intensify
until we grieve for all
until we believe
and act like
we really are one planet
immersed in redeeming possibility

~january 24, 2003

Verse 19

Is there any hope at all?

Question:
> Is there any hope at all
> in our present situation
> or are we but doomed
> to planetary destruction?

Answer:
> There's nothing much to offer
> except mysterious fullness
> possibility
> and creative vitality.

Response:
> Oh
> is that all?

~october 13, 2003

It is time to embrace the radical openness that charac-
terizes our universe, and the mysterious fullness that
inebriates the whole of reality: the seething energy sur-
facing from the quantum vacuum, forever begetting
novelty and vitality in a universe poised for unlimited
innovation, creative possibility, and divine exuberance.
~Diarmuid Ó Murchú (*Evolutionary Faith*, p. 56)

Reflection 18

The Best of Times in the Worst of Times

> For the first time in all of time, men have seen the earth: . . . seen it from the depths of space; seen it whole. . . . To see the earth as it truly is, small and blue and beautiful in that eternal silence where it floats, is to see ourselves as riders on the earth together, brothers on that bright loveliness in the eternal cold – brothers who know now they are truly brothers. **~Archibald MacLeish** (reflections on first pictures of earth from the moon, *The New York Times*, December 25, 1968, p. 1)

BIG QUESTIONS ARE SHAKING OUR HUMAN FOUNDATIONS. No institution, culture, religious tradition, community, or human is exempt from the questioning: Is our universe really 13.89 billion-years-old and our earth 4.6 billion-years-old? Are humans better than any other part of creation? Are we really destroying the planet irreparably? Do all creatures have rights? Are we all responsible for the rise of terrorism? Why is fundamentalism on the rise globally? Why do we tolerate racial cleansing? Why will we not be prepared when we run out of oil? Why are we allowing HIV/AIDS to kill as many as we killed in wars during the last century? Why can't we control drugs? Why are we spending ever more money on prisons, law enforcement, and militarism? Why isn't education solving our deepest problems? With our developed economic and political systems, why are so many people getting poorer? Why does economic and political security not bring real happiness?

If we are so evolved, why these questions, which become spirit questions when they threaten our operating worldview and threaten our basic life relationships. Today, threats are blowing our worldviews and systems to smithereens, and in the process sometimes transforming them.

The transition from the pre-modern to modern era was overwhelming, but not as overwhelming as the transition from the modern to the post-modern. I date the beginning of the post-modern era to the early 20th century, about 1916 on, after Einstein's general theory of relativity. His new picture of the universe has had revolutionary effect upon our history, born out in the Big Bang theory, the atomic bomb, quantum physics, not to mention focusing us on and sending us into outer space.

We are being bombarded with global images and planetary challenges with no place to hide – everyone knows what is happening and that dreaded crises are happening sooner rather than later. Because change is coming faster and its effects are broadcast so widely and quickly, our global consciousness intensifies exponentially. Consider the consequences of this list of what's happened in the last century or less:

- *World wars*: 100 million killed in 20th century wars/ military buildup globally
- *Global terrorism*: especially since September 11, 2001
- *Global polity*: some 200 nations/ UN/ tribunals/ protests against "globalization"
- *Global economy*: corporations/ WTO/ International Monetary Fund/ G8/ NAFTA/ European Union
- *Global ecological issues*: global warming/ sustainable resources/ oil consumption/ water rights
- *Global advertising*: on TV at Olympics and Academy Awards/ PR industry
- *Global space exploration*: satellites/ Hubble space telescope/ space stations

- *International pandemics*: HIV/AIDS/ war on drugs/ SARS
- *International care projects*: disaster relief/ international aid
- *Global research*: medical/ atmospheric/ biospheric/ Human Genome Project
- *International education*: exchange students/ international terms/ cyber-education
- *International travel*: tourism industry/ business travel
- *Global communications:* radio/ television/ media/ tele-communications
- *World Wide Web*: digital related interchange
- *International sports*: Olympics/ soccer
- *International art*: movies/ popular music/ exhibits
- *Global icons*: Earthrise image/ Moon landing
- *Universe story*: epic narrative of the nearly 14 billion years of our universe
- *Global spiritual interchange*: interfaith dialogue/ over 2000 religious groups

Such a list helps us see that we are in a new world compared with the world of my great-grandparents, who died at the beginning of the 20th century. During the post-modern era, our global culture has shifted politically, economically, and culturally in the lifetime of my grandparents, parents, my wife and me, our sons, and our grandchildren.

The whole world has become ours, whether we like it or not. Undeniably this is the way it is, ever since we all saw our one blue Earth in space during the summer of 1969. The shift in consciousness intensifies no matter how we continue denying the reality that we are one. Our separateness as cultures, religions, nations, and communities intensifies, but in the big picture our drive to be separate is a desperate holdout in light of the truth of our oneness.

Our joint local-global stewardship is not just a good idea but survival-oriented. Oil production, for example, which is as much about the future of global terrorism and the equitable distribution of resources as it is about environmental pollution, has everything to do with the future of the globe. In our mindless desire for private, freewheeling transportation, with all the bells and whistles, we gluttonously devour natural resources, bring the globe to the brink of a real world war, and smother each other and the planet with a warming trend that dooms. Yet, we basically deny it and even accelerate our consumption.

If oil consumption does surpass oil production during the next decade or so, as predicted, how will we survive and who will war with whom for the dwindling reserves? It is very clear that few of our leaders will touch these issues in any substantive, future-oriented way, lest they end up like Jimmy Carter, out of office. Let us admit we are one global reality in a gargantuan oil squeeze that will radically change all our present modes of life as much when we start cutting back on oil consumption as when we started using it so recklessly during the last century.

What about the new systems needed for our living on this one planet? Are we playing tiddledywinks with our economic, political, and judicial systems? Besides global warming, how do we begin to hold the transnational corporations accountable? How do we make sure Indonesia, that obviously has the resources to make it, does make it? Then what about all those that don't seem to have the resources to make it: Afghanistan, Madagascar, Somalia, and Haiti? Just let them what? It is our planet's problem and, thus, our problem. And how do we begin to understand that we cannot sustain the present global trend of the some 85 percent poor humans wanting what the 15 percent rich humans have, not to mention what the 0.1 percent have: the 7 million millionaires on the planet.

What's going on? How did we let things get so out of balance? "Globalization" protests contend that the power of the rich, through transnational corporations, governments, and financial institutions, widens the gap between rich and poor. As my friend George Holcombe says, we must be about demythologizing capitalism as well as our religions.

We are getting very clear that new global systems are demanded. What global system can we devise for the new global plague of HIV/AIDS? Will we have to let a 100 million of our brothers and sisters and children die of this disease before the globe takes it seriously?

The new global understanding of the next leap in global ethical systems and action is becoming clear: we will all make it together or go down together. More than ever we know that the bell tolls for all of us when it tolls for any of us. We are separate yet bound. Like never before we know that the longer we let local-global inequity go unchecked, the wider and deeper it touches all of us physically, emotionally, and spiritually.

Global terrorism has come into its own now that it's come to the "developed" nations. What a century we have before us. Will the wars of the 20th century be put to shame as terrorists' slingshots take on the military armadas of an international coalition? Authentic reflection has begun on terrorism and its root causes: "Avoiding Armageddon," the eight-hour series during April on PBS television is a powerful example.

When we remember our global *angst* around September 11, we are clear that terror anywhere, perpetrated by a few, makes peace fragile everywhere for all 6.4 billion humans. We are all suffering in this global community, despite economic status, religion, education, color, sex, or species. We all have reason to be insecure no matter where we live. We all exploit as well as sustain, consume as well as save, use as well as serve, compete as well as cooperate. We know, deep down, that if we change our priorities and redirect our will, we can kill hunger, pollution, homelessness, joblessness, disease, and illiteracy, rather than kill each other within our planetary community.

We are all beginning to see that we are not only our sister's keeper but our polar bear's keeper. No matter how we slice it, our number-one priority is care for the earth community, with all its species, including the human. We are getting clear that our life together depends on the future of mountains, tundra, forests, marine/islands, deserts, grasslands, and savannas, which are fast becoming ghosts of earth's once resplendent biosphere. We sat in pain as we digested the tragic facts from the PBS special "Bill Moyers Reports: Earth on Edge" and listened to his closing words:

> I take from what these scientists are telling us that we're on the edge of the greatest challenge humanity has ever confronted. . . . Some of them think the next three decades will be make or break. Thirty years are what we have; they say, thirty years to transform our relationship to the natural world; thirty years to reverse long standing patterns of production and consumption; thirty years to learn how to take care of the ecosystems that sustain us.

It's hard to hide anymore. Obviously, we stockholders of planet earth need to protect more than the bottom-lines of transnational corporations and to pay off more than our national and personal debts. Denial is strong but our consciousness is catching up with reality. We are not quitting. Integrated global priorities of many global groups and citizens proliferate for a viable future for the planet, down to implementing steps. Slowly we are coming to our senses, starting to care for the whole garden and all its beings, lest paradise becomes a dump.

We are beginning to understand that the next seven generations are our responsibility, or that whatever goes extinct will not ever come back again. We are getting clear that we are stewards of creation, and that our opportunities to serve have never been greater. In spite of all, I still believe we all have more of a propensity toward communion than violence. Therefore, in these worst of times we are all together in the great work of caring for the beings of the whole earth and its atmosphere.

We humans are beginning to move beyond denial, and, along with real leaders, we will face the truth and do what needs to be done. We humans are beginning to move into our true future and move out of Babel's lust. Will the move happen in my lifetime? It has begun.

Astronaut Rusty Schweikart helps us to see what is:

> When you go around the Earth in an hour and half, you begin to recognize that your identity is with the whole thing. . . . You look down there and you can't imagine how many borders and boundaries you cross, again and again and again, and you don't even see them. There you are – hundreds of people in the Middle East killing each other over some imaginary line that you're not even aware of, that you can't see. And from where you see it, the thing is a whole, the earth is a whole, and it's so beautiful. You wish you could take a person in each hand, one from each side in the various conflicts, and say, "Look. Look at it from this perspective. Look at that. What's important?" (*No Frames, No Boundaries*)

The best of times in the worst of times is calling forth those who honor all creation, not just the self, family, community, tribe – or not just the human species.

"All the Earth belongs to all" is our liberating mantra. "Belongs" and "all" are the key words: "*all* the earth *belongs* to *all*" – not to just humans and not to just rich humans. This mantra will transform humanism and socialism. Mother Earth is not our possession but belongs to all as riders together on her/our bright blue loveliness.

129

Our Home Sweet Home

Earth is not just a planet
not just a place in space
"x" distance from here and there

Our home is the earth
the place where our heart is
there's no place like home

Earth is trillions of home-ones
who live and have their being
on and in her wondrous realm

Lord knows we love our home
sustained and united in her kingdom
of communion one with the other

But we feel threatened of late
by our disregard for the way
we have treated our mother

Thus many are losing their home
many are being denied her riches
many are being denied their birthright

As all her children we dare to see
what's happening to our kin
and are beginning to grieve and act

For we know deep down
that if more and more lose their home
earth for all of us is threatened

But we *can* go home again
if we love mother earth
and find our fulfillment in her's

So let's sing with Irving

God bless our planet earth
Home that we love
Be within her and guide her
Through the night with the light from above

From the ozone to the humans
To the oceans white with foam
God bless our planet earth
Our home sweet home

God bless our planet earth
Our home sweet home

~march 2, 2003

131

Exercise 21

Who Is My Neighbor?

1. My biggest neighbor is

2. My smallest neighbor is

3. My farthest neighbor is

4. My oldest neighbor is

5. My neighbor I can't do without is

6. My most caring neighbor is

7. My neighbor that delights me most is

8. My meanest neighbor is

9. My most fragile neighbor is

10. My most abused neighbor is

11. My most needy neighbor is

12. The neighbor most on my mind is

13. The neighbors I will help this year are

14. Summary statement: My neighbor is

~january 2003

Reflection 19

Who Is My Neighbor
2000 Years Later*

> And he [legal expert] answered, "You are to love the Lord your God . . . and your neighbor as yourself." Jesus said to him, "You have given the correct answer; do this and you will have life." But with a view to justifying himself, he said to Jesus, "But who is my neighbor."
> **~Luke 10:27-29** (*The Five Gospels*, p. 323)

MOST CHRISTIANS have heard a sermon with the title "Who Is My Neighbor?" citing this text, for it highlights Jesus' first and second commandment: "love God . . . and love the neighbor." These are the basics of Christianity and its ethics, as it emerged out of Judaism. To move into the new era we have to re-understand the basics of "neighbor": no longer just a *man* in a ditch who has been beaten up and left to die, but more like a total earth community lying there.

Who is my neighbor? is not a question for us in the context of 2000 years ago, but today. The neighbor is not just family and friends, nearby neighbors, people at work, people in our organizations. And the neighbor is not just human beings. I am my neighbor. My tribe is my neighbor. 6 billion humans are my neighbor. The earth is my neighbor. Everything in creation is my neighbor.

Maybe we can use a phrase like the big neighbor, or the "Neighbor" with a capital "N," for the good creation, which includes all the species – especially the ones nearing extinction, like the honey bee and earth's old forests.

Today, when I experience myself numb with anxiety over the dying earth, I remember my anxiety as a boy growing up under the mushroom threat of the atomic bomb. Just this week the UN came out with its third report on environmental trends, wherein over 1,000 scientists and a host of international research centers and agencies said, "Without the environment, there can never be the kind of development needed to secure a fair deal for this or future generations." Was the spokesperson even talking about the future generations of all species, or mostly about the future of the human species?

What about the atmosphere that affects what's happening with the Arctic and Antarctic meltdowns and consequently what's happening with the Pacific island nation of Tuvalu, where all the residents are being forced to consider moving off their nine islands because of rising ocean waters caused by global warming?

By the way, there are plenty of well-educated folks who are saying, "All that global warming stuff is a bunch of hooey." Though we disagree, they are our neighbors, and we must find a way to dialogue.

I am not giving just a current account of who the neighbor is. St. Francis knew the big Neighbor back in the 13th century. Listen again to his well-known lines:

> All creatures of our God and King . . .
> O brother sun . . . O sister moon . . .
> O brother wind, air, clouds, and rain . . .
> Thou rising morn . . . ye lights of evening . . .
> O sister water . . . O brother fire . . .
> Dear mother Earth . . .
> The flowers and fruits . . .
> Our sister, gentle death . . .
> Let all things their Creator bless. . . .

Francis was rehearsing the litany of the good creation, which includes us humans.

As Thomas Berry says, there is not just suicide and genocide (human killing) going on, there is also biocide and geocide (earth killing) going on. Whose Constitution gives rights to the non-humans? Which newspapers publish the obituaries for the 29,000 species that die each year?

On our shrinking globe we are charged to take care of all the neighbors, for as the earth neighborhood goes, so goes me and my house. This is one of the big lessons of September 11. Care of the earth community is not just a good idea, it's also about our personal survival as humans.

I think Jesus and Abraham are speaking to us today through St. Francis and Thomas Berry, as well as through Gandhi and MLK, Jr., and Archbishop Tutu – not only to take care of the human neighbor but also to take care of the non-human neighbor.

As the earth goes, so we humans go. To update John Donne's poem, "No human is an island, entire of itself; every human is a piece of the planet, a part of the universe; if soil be washed away because of no trees, we all are the less; any species' death diminishes me; and therefore never send to know for whom the bell tolls; it tolls for thee" – it tolls for all. We are not only our brother's keeper, we are our river's keeper, for we are commissioned to be good stewards of creation.

Our sense of "neighbor" is human-centered. Even "Do unto others . . ." is a rehearsal of our human-centered contradiction until we understand "others" to mean "all others" in our earth community, not just human beings. Maybe we can symbolize our transition into the new era by simply adding to this great human mantra the word "all": "Do unto *all* others as you would have them do unto you" – at least the whole earth community and its ozone layer. Only then do we begin to understand what "love the neighbor" means today.

We are all the good creation, all interconnected. Let me say that again: we are all the good creation. Cuba is loved as much as the USA. And I do not presume that any deity loves me any more than it loves the dying honey bee. We are all neighbors put here to care for one another. If we wipe out any part of creation, the rest of creation suffers eventually.

The philosopher is right: "I am myself *and* what is around me, and if I do not save it, it will not save me" (José Ortega y Gasset, 1914). And the poet is right: "A culture is no better than its woods" (W.H. Auden, *"Woods," Selected Poetry, p. 146*) and "We must love one another or die" (W.H. Auden, "September 1, 1939," from *Another Time*) I want to make sure Auden's poetry includes the non-human as well as the human. I therefore say it this way: a culture is no better than its oppressed – its woods and its poor. We must all love each other or die.

Where do I decide to draw the line of who is and who is not my neighbor? How do we decide which neighbor to love next and most? These are the right questions. But we mustn't stop with questions. Like the Samaritan in Jesus' parable, we must directly engage to help the human and the non-human dying in the ditch beside the road. It's a matter of strategic, loving service.

Who is my neighbor? We spent those billions of dollars as U.S. citizens to send our astronauts to the Moon back in 1969 to take a photo of planet Earth. We now have the picture of the Neighbor, the big blue marble flung out there in our glorious universe. Ignorance is no longer an excuse.

Hear this prayer of gratitude (UN service of "Earth Rest Day," June 1-3, 1990, adapted) for the Big Neighbor.

> We rejoice in all . . . [creation]
> We live in all things

All things live in us
We live by the sun
We move with the stars
We eat from the earth
We drink from the rain
We breathe from the air
We share with all creatures
We have . . . strength from their gifts . . .
We . . . [care with them]
We . . . [celebrate with them]
We are [all] full of the grace of creation
We are grateful . . .
We rejoice in . . . [the good creation.] [**Amen.**]

As Auden says, "we must love each other or die." That's the judgment. As grace would have it, in loving God and all others we have life.

> . . . And the legal expert answered, "You are to love the Lord your God . . . and your neighbor as yourself." Jesus said to him, "You have given the correct answer; do this and you will have life."

Again, in loving God and all others we will have life. This is the good news on this day in May.
So be it.
Be it so.

*Adapted from talk given at Seigle Avenue Presbyterian Church, Charlotte, North Carolina, May 26, 2002.

Verse 22 *My Neighbor Is*

My biggest neighbor is Grandfather Universe
My smallest neighbor is Little Neutrino
My oldest and farthest neighbor is Old Fireball
My neighbor I can't do without is Father Sun
My most caring neighbor is Mother Earth
My most delightful neighbors are Nolan and Kaitlyn
My meanest neighbors are War and Poverty
My most fragile neighbor is Uncle Water
My most abused neighbor is Teen Prostitute
My most needy neighbor is HIV/AIDS Millions
My neighbor most on my mind is Dispirited Masses

Whatever I do not do for the least of these . . .

If we say we love God and hate the neighbor, we
are liars . . .

> The second is like unto the first . . .
> And thy neighbor as thyself . . .

One fell among thieves and was dying in a ditch
> Two holy ones saw him and passed by
> His enemy stopped and cared for him
> Which one was the neighbor

The earth is the Lord's and everything in it
Who can think of anything that's not the neighbor
Today I will make an offering to Brother Rain Forest
Tomorrow I will march in the streets for Sister Peace
The next day I'll meet New Folks next door

~january 17, 2003

Reflection 20

I Don't Agree With You on This One

WIFE LYNDA IS SO SOFT-SPOKEN AND KIND, but sometimes she steps up with megaphone to defend the pluriformity of the 6.4 billion human creatures. She received the following e-mail from a old friend on July 9, 2003, a couple of years later than the issuance of the first EID greeting stamp. (One can read right wing background on the debate by Paul M. Weyrich, Chairman of the Free Congress Foundation.) The e-mail included the picture of the second printed EID stamp for commemorating the two main Muslim holy days of over 7 million Muslims in the United States. Previous U.S. Postal Service stamps in the Holiday Celebrations are Hanukkah, Kwanzaa, and Cinco de Mayo.

The e-mail under the picture of the stamp read:

REMEMBER the MUSLIM bombing of PanAm
   Flight 103!
REMEMBER the MUSLIM bombing of the World
   Trade Center in 1993!
REMEMBER the MUSLIM bombing of the Marine
   barracks in Lebanon!
REMEMBER the MUSLIM bombing of the military
   barracks in Saudi Arabia!
REMEMBER the MUSLIM bombing of the
   American Embassies in Africa!
REMEMBER the MUSLIM bombing of the USS
   COLE!

REMEMBER the MUSLIM attack on the Twin
Towers on 9/11/2001!
REMEMBER all the AMERICAN lives that were
lost in those vicious MUSLIM attacks!

The United States Postal Service REMEMBERS
and honors the EID MUSLIM holiday season
with a commemorative first class holiday
postage stamp.
REMEMBER to adamantly and vocally BOYCOTT
this stamp when purchasing your stamps at the
post office. To use this stamp would be a slap in
the face to all those AMERICANS who died at
the hands of those whom this stamp honors.
REMEMBER to pass this along to every patriotic
AMERICAN you know.

Most of Lynda's kind but forceful e-mail follows:

Dear _____,

. . . I don't agree with you on this one. . . . Some
dear friends and acquaintances of mine are
Muslims. They are kind and thoughtful and generous. I
don't think badly of them because of what a few people
of their religion did, just as I hope someone doesn't
think badly of me because of what some other white
Christians did in history.

I've just finished reading *My Traitor's Heart*, by
Rian Malan, about apartheid in South Africa. The
treatment of the blacks by the S.A. white Christians is
appalling, but it was not all white Christians in South
Africa, and hardly all white Christians in the world.

The way I see it, if we are ever to have peace and
reconciliation in this world, we must not put blanket
condemnation on one group of people over another. We
must find ways to reach out in care and concern to show

that we are willing to try to understand the others' points of view and be open to their religious understandings, regardless of what a few of that religion have done. It would be like saying that all white Christians are to be shunned because of the actions of a few who brought hundreds of thousands of Africans to America to be sold as slaves.

When we lived in Indonesia, with over a 90 percent Muslim population, we attended worship at a few local mosques with Muslim friends. We were astonished to see the same Old Testament stories in their tradition as in ours. We attended several of their feast days, one of which is commemorated by the EID stamp. We were there when the goats were sacrificed, as they rehearsed the Abraham story. . . . I was awestruck.

We were so cautious about singing Christmas carols the first year we were there because we were so visible in a small Muslim village. However, one of the village leaders came up to us and said, "We know this is your special time of the year. Please go ahead with your celebrations. . . ."

We have a few Muslim children in the school where I teach now. We were very sensitive for a few weeks about any discrimination toward them after 9/11. Later in the year, when we were doing holidays from around the world, we invited the mother of one to come to our class and tell us a bit about their tradition. She wore the traditional head covering and explained it to the children. She brought a Koran and special treats that they serve during the holy days. . . . The children were very responsive.

To me, the stamp is a great idea. There are millions of Muslims in this country. We have all kinds of stamps to choose from. We have stamps of cars, and cars kill people each day. I would buy the EID stamp as one small symbol of being open to the Rainbow World in which we live. To me, it certainly doesn't have anything to do with supporting a small group of people's

141

bad and evil choices.

Hope you will receive this in the spirit of reconciliation in which I send it,

Lynda

The story does not end here. The friend who sent the
"Remember e-mail" read Lynda's and replied: "Thank you,
Lynda, for the different approach and thoughts. I am
forwarding this on to everyone I sent the original one to.
Please accept it in the open-minded way I am sending it."

Then Lynda replied again:

Thank you for your nice reply. We are all so careless
about things that could hurt other people, without really
meaning to. I used to tell "Polock" jokes until my niece
married a young man from Poland. When I met his
parents, who barely escaped from Hitler's regime with
their lives, I was sorry for having taken another group
of people so lightly. I keep learning.

Authentic dialogue was going on here. We are all called to
be agents of reconciliation on this journey. Lynda has
certainly taken that calling to heart in small and large ways.
Reconciliation seldom happens without risks, either small
or big.

E 23 *My Vocation Exercise . . .*

1. Difference between "career/job" and "vocation" is

   _____

2. Words I associate with "vocation" are

   _____

3. Yes or No: I have experienced one vocational call
   (when: _____)

4. Yes or No: I have experienced many vocation calls.

5. Yes or No: I can retire from my vocation.

6. A vocated person in history we all know of was (is)

   _____

7. The most vocated person I have known personally

   _____

8. "Vocation" for a person on the spirit journey is about

   _____

9. The situations begging for my vocational response
   these days are

   · _____
   · _____
   · _____
   · _____

10. At this moment, the dates for my burial marker/
    obituary are 19___-2___; my 5-7 word *epitaph*
    (what epitomizes a deceased person's life) for my
    burial marker/obituary (e.g., "S/he cared for
    _____ ")

11. My vocation or life's work is

_____

12. Practically, through my vocation I intend to

_____

13. My statement of vocation follows:

Reflection 21

Human Development Recontexted

"I doubt, therefore, I am,"
Said René Descartes,
Letting loose Western humanism.

But what about
"I dialogue, therefore, I am";
"I care, therefore, I am"?

Or what about
"I commune, therefore, I am";
"I intercommune, therefore, I am"?

In any case, I am I,
In relationship with all that is,
I have no doubt.

WITH AN OVEREMPHASIS on the human's place in creation, especially over the some four-hundred years since Descartes, we are now moving into an age of emphasis on creation as a whole, even if much too slowly.

We have begun to realize the big and rightful context for who we are as humans. Rather than operating as though we are the reason why creation began in the first place, and rather than focusing our best attention and efforts on human and self-development, we are becoming more aware of our oneness with and our responsibility for creation. We are maturing, even if much too slowly.

We are being reminded that oneness, awareness, possibility, mercy, grace, peace, hope, joy, meaning – the real stuff of life – are not the product of human ingenuity and decision but free gifts from the heart of creation.

Human development is an illusion if we think that human fulfillment is in our hands. Sure, some of what we call human development is in our hands; therefore, we undergo education, training, and sensitizing. But we should know by now that education, economics, and politics are not the final answer to human development on the planet. Getting rich does not fulfill or make us happy. Getting an education does not make us happy. Getting a democratic system of government does not make us happy, finally.

At the same time, education, economics, and politics are means we can use to relate more authentically with creation. For example, we can educate for planetary health, we can budget for planetary health, and we can govern for planetary health. Human development makes sense only within the context of planetary development. Our mission to care for the earth and all of her species, biomes, and her atmosphere fulfills us deeply, and helps create the environment for a healthier future life on this planet for all its inhabitants.

Therefore, focusing on the health of the planet rather than the health of a nation – or my personal health – is the new context that can deliver liberty and justice for all. The human venture is meant to be lived out within the context of the earth venture. This is the new world order.

I'm not saying human development is out. I'm simply saying that what we mean by human development needs a radically different context. We humans are an important part of the universe, but not indispensable. Earth got along without us for most of its history and can for the rest of it.

Yet, here we are, with a crucial and great work to do. Instead of the old context with humans at the center, consider this simple and easy-to-remember "I-Thee" acronym for our relational place within the universe.

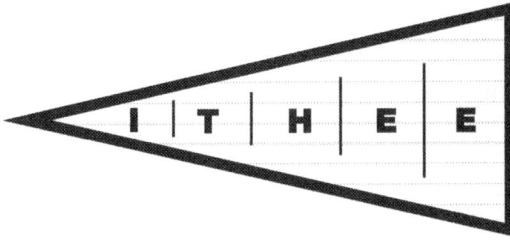

I-THEE Context

I: "I" is certainly part of the context of human development but is not its center. This is fundamental to a new understanding for human development. The human "I" is physical and biological, conscious, and spiritual by nature. "I" is a journeyer by nature – all "I's" have a story line of past, present, and future. "I" cares by its nature – all "I's" care for something beyond self. "I" is therefore relational to all others.

T: "Tribe" stands for all the interrelationships of all the "I's," from immediate family and associations to one's regional, religious, and cultural bloc, e.g., "European"; "Native American"; "Arab." These are our traditional relationships of care.

H: "Humanity" stands for all the rest, all the 6.4 billion human beings alive on the planet. These too are natural relationships of care, though not as close as the tribe.

E: "Earth" stands for the whole earth community in her connectedness, all species. Although the earth community has been a mutual relationship for humans in the past, it has become less so today, especially for urban dwellers.

E: "Everything" stands for everything else, i.e., other planets, solar system, galaxies, dark matter. As we peer into and even reside in outer space, how do we relate to all that as earthlings?

Then, human and self-development are rightly understood within the context of all creation. Are we humans significant and vital to creation? Of course. Are we the quintessence of creation? No more than anything else. We are all the quintessence of creation.

Martin Buber's I-Thou concept stimulates the I-THEE Context. As he says, we have the possibility of treating any other as a *thou*, reverently as a subject, rather than an *it*, or an object to be used. All creation, not only humans, deplores being used. Usury is against the law of the universe. India's greeting of "namaste" is an example of bowing to the other, all others, as a *thou*, seeing all others as sacred and thereby mirroring to us our own sacredness.

The question arises, Where is the eternal *thou*, or *spirit*, in this I-THEE Context? Is *spirit* beyond *everything*? No, that would be falling back into the old notion of another realm outside creation, something metaphysical, which hardly makes sense to us today.

The two acronyms used earlier answer the question Where is *spirit*?

- SEP: "*spirit's* ever-present"
- SATH: "*spirit's* at the heart"

Spirit is throughout the diagram – represented by the lines permeating all parts of the I-THEE Context – because *spirit's* at the heart of creation. As said in the introduction, because creation is one big set of relations, *spirit* is happening all the time and everywhere. *Spirit* happens in relationship.

All of this said, a big part of the great work of us humans – and us authors – is to help other humans to understand this expanded context of creation development and care, which makes sense of human and self-development. This is nothing new, but obviously something new for us humans alive today.

148

Verse 24

Humanism Is Bust

Merriam and Webster define a "humanist" as one who is
concerned about . . .
> the humanities
> literary culture
> individual dignity and worth
> self-realization through reason
> a critical spirit
> secular concerns characterized by the Renaissance
> philosophy viewed non-theistically
> and humanitarian efforts.

This is all well and good, and a bit highfalutin.

But what about their other meaning of "humanism" wherein
one is concerned about . . .
> a doctrine, attitude, or way of life centered on
>   human interests or values?

Haven't we done this definition to death?
Hasn't our human-centeredness turned in on us?
Haven't our obsessive human interests and values
terribly tinkered with the planet?

One more meaning they give about "humanism" . . .
> a philosophy that usually rejects supernaturalism.

What does humanism put in supernaturalism's place?
Not much.

How do humanists talk about
the height and depth of human experience?
Their jargon seems flat, without much sap.
Whose philosophy is deeply satisfying
the soul of us humans these days?

"Humanism" is bust,
the worst of the "-isms,"
and Earth's major contradiction.

What about the words
"humanist" and "humanistic"?
Like father like son.

Coin new words
for creation's sake!
Webster and Merriam,
            re-ink your quills.

~august 13, 2003

Reflection 22

The Creation-centered Revolution

A human being is a part of a whole called by us "the universe." . . . He experiences himself, his thoughts and feelings, as something separate from the rest – a kind of optical illusion of his consciousness. This delusion is a kind of prison for us, restricting us to our personal desires and affection for a few persons nearest to us. Our task must be to free us from this prison by widening our circle of understanding and compassion to embrace all living creatures and the whole of nature.*

~Albert Einstein (*Exp. Quotable Einstein,* p. 316)

At sunset of the third day, near the village of Igendja, we moved along an island set in the middle of the wide river. On a sandbank to our left, four hippopotamuses and their young plodded along in our same direction. Just then, in my great tiredness and discouragement, the phrase, "Reverence for Life," struck me like a flash. . . . Now I knew that a system of values which concerns itself only with our relationship to other people is incomplete. . . . Only by means of reverence for life can we establish a spiritual and humane relationship with both people and all living creatures.

~Albert Schweitzer ("A. S. Speaks Out")

HUMAN-CENTEREDNESS, with its Enlightenment focus on human progress, is giving way to *creation-centeredness.* The revolution set off by Copernicus in the 16th century changed two things fundamentally: one, our would-be human-controlled planet Earth was no longer the center of the universe; second, we of Western civilization crawled out from under the authority of the church and began to think independently. But the scientific-technological breakloose that has grown out of the second change convinces us humans that we are still the center of creation.

Not a day goes by that I don't encounter myself being human-centered in my thinking, organization, and action. Our human-centeredness speaks to our overemphasis on human wishes and needs. But we will not fulfill humanity by fixating on humanity any more than we will fulfill the self by fixating on the self. The universe does not operate myopically. Biospheric alerts clarify that we humans cannot have what we want and need, in the long run, apart from what the earth wants and needs.

We are living in deep illusion if we think human development, in and of itself, is the primary purpose of creation. If our sense of reality is focused upon the human journey apart from the earth and universe journeys, and if we do not take most seriously the power at the heart of the one journey, we are surely doomed. The one journey of all in the universe is the very truth that compels us to take the next creational leap: our purpose as the human community is to give ourselves willingly to and for the common, immense journey of creation. We are still in the midst of the first part of the Copernican revolution, but we are beginning to get the point, finally: the universe is *the thing* and we humans are a part of the universe.

In the next paragraph, after the one quoted above, Schweitzer wrote

> It also became clear to me that this elemental but complete system of values [reverence for life] possessed an altogether different depth and an entirely different vitality than one that concerned itself only with human beings. Through reverence for life, we come into *a spiritual relationship with the universe*. The inner depth

of feeling we experience through it gives us the will and the capacity to create a spiritual and ethical set of values that enable us to act on a higher plane, because we then feel ourselves truly at home in our world. Through reverence for life, *we become, in effect, different persons.* ("Albert Schweitzer Speaks Out")

Schweitzer's words are foundational for the creation-centered revolution taking place amongst us humans, the one we are trying to articulate meaningfully. I hear him saying we humans, with this new and biggest context, will find out what it means to be human in deeper ways. We will begin to understand ourselves as one universe body and will become motivated to act spontaneously on behalf of our one universe "home." Our operating image will move from human-centered to creation-centered, growing out of our "spiritual relationship with the universe."

Reverence for creation has happened to all of us, in small ways at least: lying on our backs looking at the stars, catching fireflies, snuggling up during a thunderstorm, smelling a rose on the dining room table, working in the garden, helping deliver a calf, pitching hay, going to the beach, going to the mountains, watching a sunset, experiencing a natural catastrophe, rafting, fishing, and on and on.

During such awesome times, we have experienced the great communion with the universe and its diverse family, experiencing wonder at the mystery of creation. I think this is what Schweitzer was getting at with a "spiritual relationship with the universe." As the universe communes with us intimately, we sometimes experience oneness. We get related authentically and take a new relation to our care for creation. This is not a moral victory. It is a *spirit* happening teaching us that we are at home in the universe and that she is our family. She takes care of us and we will take care of her. Through such communion with the universe the revolution is birthed in us.

Something further may happen on our revolutionary journey toward care of creation. Along the way, our deep relation with creation is deeply offended, like when we see a bird drenched in oil lying on the coast, or our beach house foundations are washed out by rising tides, or we find out our water source is unfit to drink because of runoff. Something happens to trigger our passion and we charge out the door of our comfortable, human-centered existence and begin to look for effective ways to deal with the rampant depletion of the earth's resources and the imminent death of too many of her species.

This deeper passion is showing up in more and more of us. The movement to care for creation is accelerating, even beginning to change the human-centered structures of locality, bioregion, nation, and globe. So be it. "We become, in effect, different persons." That is what a creation-centered revolution means, tens of millions of changed persons joining together to put creation first.

One last point comes out of Schweitzer's first quote: "Only by means of reverence for life can we establish a spiritual and humane relationship with both people and all living creatures" within our reach. This says to me that the creation-centered revolution will give us a deeper and more comprehensive relationship with other humans as well. Why? Because we will see humans also as a part of creation that elicits our reverence.

Thankfully, more and more of us human-centered and self-centered humans, like Schweitzer, are being healed in the process of creation's flow down the middle of the wide river, sometimes in a flash, even in great tiredness and discouragement, while four hippopotamuses and their young look on.

And, thankfully, more and more of us human-centered and self-centered humans, like Schweitzer, are therefore being healed of our separation "from the rest [of creation] – a kind of optical illusion of [our] consciousness," as Einstein says in the beginning quote. The truth is, we are "part of the whole," of the universe, of creation.

> Our task must be to free us from this prison [of human-centeredness] by widening our circle of understanding and compassion to embrace all living creatures and the whole of nature.

This transformation from our illusory human-centered consciousness to a creation-centered consciousness is the revolution we are now in. It can open the prison gates.

---

*This quote from *The Expanded Quotable Einstein* is attributed to Einstein.

Verse 25

Beatitudes

Many say . . .

Blessed are the rich
Blessed are the powerful
Blessed are the winners
Blessed are the armed
Blessed are the comfortable
Blessed are the consumers
Blessed are the entertained
Blessed are the educated
      the developed
      the civilized
      the cultured
For they inherit their self-made kingdom

But Jesus said . . .

Blessed are the poor
Blessed are the meek
Blessed are the merciful
Blessed are the pure in heart
Blessed are the peacemakers
Blessed are they that mourn
Blessed are the enemy
Blessed are those like little children
Blessed are those who do my father's will
Blessed are they that lay down their lives for others
For their kingdom is heaven on earth

I Say . . .

Blessed are all the children
      all beings
      human or not
Blessed are they
      not because of what they own
      not because of what they achieve
      but because they just are
      – each of value as it is –
Blessed are they
For they *are already* the good creation

~march 1, 2003

Reflection 23

The Next Evolutionary Leap

HAVE YOU HEARD THE STORY about your early ancestor? Not Christopher Columbus, not Abraham of Ur, not even a 60,000-year-old Aborigine of Australia. Further back. Not the 1.75 million-year anthropological find in the nation of Georgia during July. Not even Lucy of Ethiopia (a 3.2 million-year find), nor the latest find in northern Chad, also during July, a human dating back 7 million years. None of these. This ancestor goes back much, much farther. So close your eyes, breath deeply, be still as a rock, and listen with the ears of an elephant.

> There were strange . . . [creatures] in those waters, strange barbels nuzzling the bottom ooze, and there was time . . . but mostly, I think, it was the ooze. By day the temperature in the world outside the pond rose to a frightful intensity; at night the sun went down in smoking red. Dust storms marched in incessant progression across a wilderness whose plants were the plants of long ago. Leafless and weird and stiff they lingered by the water, while over vast areas of grassless uplands the winds blew until red stones took on the polish of reflecting mirrors. There was nothing to hold the land in place. Winds howled, dust clouds rolled, and brief erratic torrents choked with silt ran down to the sea. It was a time of dizzying contrasts, a time of change.
> On the oily surface of the pond, from time to time, a snout thrust upward, took in air with a queer grunting

159

inspiration, and swirled back to the bottom. The pond was doomed, the water was foul, and the oxygen almost gone, but the . . . [Snout] would not die. It could breathe air directly through a little accessory lung, and it could walk. In all that weird and lifeless landscape, it was the only thing that could. It walked rarely and under protest, but that was not surprising. The creature was a fish.

In the passage of days the pond became a puddle, but the Snout survived. There was dew one dark night and a coolness in the empty stream bed. When the sun rose next morning the pond was an empty place of cracked mud, but the Snout did not lie there. He had gone. Down stream there were other ponds. He breathed air for a few hours and hobbled slowly along on the stumps of heavy fins.

It was an uncanny business if there had been anyone there to see. It was a journey best not observed in daylight, it was something that needed swamps and shadows and the touch of the night dew. It was a monstrous penetration of a forbidden element, and the Snout kept his face from the light. It was just as well, though the face should not be mocked. In three hundred million years it would be our own.

~**Loren Eiseley** (*The Immense Journey*, pp. 50-1)

You may open your eyes now, but never forget what happened that dark night when one of our primal ancestors made that evolutionary leap. If he hadn't, we wouldn't be here.

We too are living in "a time of change" – to put it mildly – also being called on to take the next evolutionary leap. We do well not to forget our 300-million-years-old ancestor, shaking off his snout-centeredness and saying, "Why is everything drying up? It's not fair. I'm tired. I'm old. I don't want to go downstream . . . but be damned if I'm going to lie here and die." So he starts hobbling to a new pond on his fins, grunting and grumbling. Keep him in your mind's eye because he's the paradigm for how the universe process has worked and will work in the future.

For example: things are going along badly for the earth community. Somehow, someone or some few get a new vantage point and can see a new possibility beyond the imminent doom. Out of that vision comes a new way – a seemingly wild experiment, like a fish walking on fins or amoeba growing hair or a cadre of humans caring for creation – that they stick back into the process. The result: history moves in a new direction. This is how change happens in the universe. The destiny of our planet and its atmosphere is always on such pioneers' shoulders.

We humans have acted like we wanted to be in charge of the earth. Well, now we are, and in a profound way, and the universe is deciding through us, among others, how to get to the next pond.

> The task before us now, if we would not perish, is to shake off our ancient prejudices and to build the earth. **~Teilhard de Chardin**
> (*Building the Earth*, p. vii)

Could these be the words to the Snout's traveling song . . . and ours? Seems as though *spirit* would have it no other way.

~august 2002

In Summary

Verse 26

Whichever

I bow to *spirit* at the heart of creation –
always already present in creation –
whether I bow to you personally,
or to my kin on this piedmont,
or to all Earth's creatures,
or Sun's zillion neutrinos.

Humans have circled up and huddled at campfires
since the last time Mars came this close to planet Earth,
sharing stories of their experience
with the micro- and macrocosm,
inventing religion
out of spirituality:

Life happens to us and we experience it,
sometimes making us conscious of our *yes* or *no*,
sometimes making us at one with *spirit*.
Down deep we all know, or can know,
that the way life is, at heart,
it is transparent to *spirit*.

Whether we have been mostly asleep or on watch,
we beings of creation have been journeyed
univers'ly by that which journeys all –
experiencing *communion,*
being at one with all,
deciding to *intercommune* –

For this purpose: that we all care for creation,
not just for self or mine, but for everything;
bowing to each as *thou* and not as *it*.
Truly, holy traditions teach
that creation is good,
meaning "heaven is in our midst."

Where will I draw the line of "Who is my neighbor?"
if all is very good and is connected,
if reverence and compassion for all
means responsibility for all –
bowing to and serving
all created heirs of *spirit*?

"The cosmos is *spirit's*, and the fullness thereof";
we who think we "love *spirit* and hate the neighbor"
forget everything is *in* creation
and forget it's all "very good,"
forget that "the second
command is like unto the first."

I will bow to *spirit* and will see creation,
or bow to creation and see through to *spirit* . . .
        whichever . . .
for *spirit's* always at the heart.

~march 28, 2003

164

Appendices

Appendix A

An Earlier Outline

THE CHART on the next two pages was an earlier outline for this book, but in the last few years I have come to see that we must strategically be about deepening spirituality rather than spreading religion. As I wrote in my last book, "rediscovering our one, universal Spirit tradition" is the necessary task. "We must go far beyond the ecumenical and interfaith activities of the past. We must claim our common Spirit journey for the sake of our common Earth future" (*Our Universal Spirit Journey*, p. 27). I agree with Diarmuid Ó Murchú when he writes,

> Spiritual engagement for our time is not about revitalising or renewing religion and its accompanying moral, dogmatic and liturgical practices. Rather, the primary task of spirituality is to enable and empower people to reclaim the fundamental *raison d'être* of all religion: the engagement with, and practical living out of, those deep values [I would prefer the word "realities"] which alone can assuage the spiritual hunger in the heart of every human being.
> (*Reclaiming Spirituality*, p. 173)

I do not fully agree with his earlier assessment of "new spirituality" that believes "religion is a temporary reality that in all probability has outlived its usefulness." However, I do not want to take more time to demythologize (or deliteralize, as Tillich says) my religion. That was part of my task in *The Transparent Event: Post-modern Christ Images*. These days I am not so much interested in discussing the differences (*continue after chart on p. 169*)

167

The Way of Intercommunion
of all things with the heart of creation

Points of Focus / From and To	Transcendent Worldview . . . From an image of . . .	Transparent Worldview . . . to an image of . . .
I. The Heart of Creation: dynamics of spirituality		
Key	Other-worldliness	Other world in this world
Source	Transcendent God	Spirit's ever-presence
Locus	Beyond everything	At the heart of everything
Eventfulness	Past and future	Now
Preoccupation	Original sin	Original goodness
II. Eventful Re-creation: dynamics of transparency		
Sin	Deeds of omission/commission	State of separation (illusion)
God	Eternal Lord	Eternal Creator
Christ	Essence of grace	Event of grace
Jesus	God	Anointed human
Holy Spirit	Miraculous power	Creative, freeing, uniting power

III. Communion with Creation: dynamics of communion		
Focus	Human-centered	Creation-centered
Scenario	Personal salvation	Universe journey
Aim	Make sense of creation	Communion with creation
Linkage	Believing	Reunion ("yes of seeing thru")
Modality	Right belief	Depth experience
IV. Reconciliation with Creation: dynamics of intercommunion		
Church	The chosen	Servant force
Emphasis	Evangelism	Reconciliation
Catalyst	Establishment led	Transestablishment inspired
Result	Exclusive communion	Acts of intercommunion
Commandment	Religion: love God	Spirituality: love Spirit's creation

between my Christ image and traditionally held images of Christ. If we are not careful, such an exercise can further divide people within a religious tradition.

I now simply want to offer practical images and exercises for a universal spirituality. Of course, my religion and others will be helpful in the process as we focus on how to relate to the heart of creation transparently manifest in the particulars of our common creation. I trust this book is another step in that direction. (Bill Salmon gave helpful input to this chart.)

Appendix B

Major Human Shifts
of the Last 70,000 Years

The debate over when humans began to look and act like us present humans is hotter than ever. When humans started symbolic thinking is far from a consensus, but I have seen dates going back 40,000 to 70,000 years Before the Common Era. I have chosen the longer time for the chart on the next page to lay out in broadest strokes our human journey into the immediate future. Those tens of thousands of years from the *early human* to us most *modern humans* brings us to entering the *ecozoic human* period, a time of intercommunion when we dramatically accelerate our care for the rest of creation, or. . . .

Appendix C

Major Human Shifts
in Western Civilization

Going from 10,000 years Before the Common Era up until the 22nd century of the Common Era, the chart, on the second page following, suggests the more or less intentional human shifts in Western civilization, meaning those human constructs built for living in the environs in which they/we have found ourselves. As we have moved through the religious and scientific stories, now we have written and have begun to read and reflect on the universe story of who we are and what we are about. Bigger shifts emerge.

Major Human Shifts of the Last 70,000 Years

Time \ Category	Economy of . . .	Politics of . . .	Culture of . . .	Spirituality of . . .
Early Human	Dependence: live and let live	Tribalism: part of the tribe	In the "environment"	Sacredness: fear and fascination
Modern Human	Independence: earth as resource	Democracy: part of the human world	Self as the center	Salvation: human fulfillment
Ecozoic Human	Interdependence: human as resource	Biocracy: part of the natural world	Everything as the center	Intercommunion: creation fulfillment

Major Shifts in Western Civilization

Category / Time	Meaning Focus	Rational Objective	Existential Aim	Historical Grounding
Pre-Modern (10,000 BCE to 1750 CE)	Human mythology — Religious story	Articulate system of meaning	Humans answer life questions	Great religions; Humanities; Temples
Modern (1750 to 1916 CE)	Human "progress" — Scientific story	Invent industrial, technological miracles	Humans rule their environment	Great inventions; Sciences; Einstein's theory
Post-Modern (1916 to 22nd cent CE)	Inter-communion — Universe story	Befriend planetary society	Humans reinvent spirit journey	Great wars; Spiritualities; Earthrise

Selected Bibliography

Auden, W. H. *Another Time*. New York: Random House, 1940.
————. *Selected Poetry*. New York: Modern Library, 1958.
Berry, Thomas, with Thomas Clarke. *Befriending the Earth*: *A Theology of Reconciliation Between Humans and the Earth*, ed. Stephen Dunn and Anne Lonergan. Mystic, Conn.: Twenty-Third, 1992.
————. *The Dream of the Earth*. 1988; San Francisco: Sierra Club, 1990.
————. *The Great Work*: *Our Way Into the Future*. New York: Random House, 1999.
————. *Thomas Berry and the New Cosmology*, ed. Anne Lonergan and Caroline Richards. Mystic, Conn.: Twenty-Third, 1991.
————. (with Brian Swimme) *The Universe Story*: *From the Primordial Flaring Forth to the Ecozoic Era – A Celebration of the Unfolding of the Cosmos*. N.Y.: HarperCollins, 1992.
Buber, Martin. *I and Thou*, trans. R. G. Smith. New York: Scribners, 1958.
————. *I and Thou*, trans. Walter Kaufmann. New York: Scribners, 1970.
Calaprice, Alice, ed. *The Expanded Quotable Einstein*. Princeton: Princeton University Press, 2000.
————. *The Quotable Einstein*. Princeton: Princeton University Press, 1996.
Cock, John P. *Called To Be*: *A Spirit Odyssey*. Greensboro, N.C.: tranScribe books, 2000.
————. *Motivation for the Great Work*: *Forty Meaty Meditations for the Secular-religious*. San Jose: Authors Choice, 2000.
————. *Our Universal Spirit Journey*: *Reflection and Verse for Creation's Sake*. Greensboro, N.C.: tranScribe books, 2002.

————. *The Transparent Event: Post-modern Christ Images.* Greensboro, N.C.: tranScribe books, 2001.

Epps, John L., gen. ed. *Bending History: Reflections of a Religious Revolutionary.* Co-eds.: Cock, John P.; Holcombe, George; Pesek, Betty C.; Walters, M. George. Pub. 2004.

Eiseley, Loren. *The Immense Journey.* New York: Vintage, 1957.

Funk, Robert W.; Hoover, Roy W.; and the Jesus Seminar. *The Five Gospels: The Search for the Authentic Words of Jesus.* New York: Macmillan, 1993.

Goodenough, Ursala. *The Sacred Depths of Nature.* New York: Oxford, 1998.

Kierkegaard, Søren. *Fear and Trembling* and *The Sickness Unto Death*, trans. Walter Lowrie. New York: Doubleday, 1954.

Lawrence, Brother. *The Practice of the Presence of God.* White Plains, N.Y.: Peter Pauper Press, 1983.

Lawrence, D. H. *The Complete Poems of D. H. Lawrence.* New York: Penguin, 1977.

Lesser, Elizabeth. *The New American Spirituality.* New York: Random House, 1999.

Merton, Thomas. *The Way of Chuang Tzu.* New York: New Directions, 1965.

Marshall, Gene W. *The Call of the Awe: Rediscovering Christian Profundity in an Interreligious Era.* Lincoln, Neb.: Writers Club Press, 2003.

Marrow, Lance. *Evil: An Investigation.* New York: Basic Books, 2003.

Nhât Hanh, Thích. *The Heart of Understanding*, ed. Peter Levitt. Berkeley: Parallax Press, 1988.

Ó Murchú, Diarmuid. *Evolutionary Faith: Rediscovering God in Our Great Story.* Maryknoll, N.Y.: Orbis Books, 2002.

————. *Reclaiming Spirituality: A New Spiritual Framework for Today's World.* 1997; N.Y.: Crossroad, 2000.

Ortega y Gasset, José. *Meditations on Quixoté.* Publicaciones Residencia de Estudias, series II, vol. 1, Madrid, 1914.

Schweickart, Russell. *No Frames, No Boundaries* (1977),

excerpted in "In Context" journal, Summer 1983, p. 16.

Schweitzer, Albert. Special Report: "Albert Schweitzer Speaks Out," the World Book Online Reference Center, http://www.worldbookonline.com, October 31, 2003. Chicago: World Book Yearbook, 1964.

———. *Out of My Life and Thought*. New York: Henry Holt, 1933.

Sharp, Basil. *The Adventure of Being Human: A Guide to Living a Fuller Life*. Washington: Integrated Life Architects, 2000.

Smith, Huston. *The Illustrated World's Religions: A Guide to Our Wisdom Tradition*. San Francisco: Harper, 1994.

Spretnak, Charlene. *States of Grace: Recovery of Meaning in the Postmodern Age*. San Francisco: HarperCollins, 1993.

Stanfield, Brian. *The Courage to Lead: Transform Self, Transform Society*. Gabriola Island, Canada: New Society, 2000.

Swimme, Brian. *The Hidden Heart of the Cosmos: Humanity and the New Story*. Maryknoll, N.Y.: Orbis, 1996.

———. (with Thomas Berry) *The Universe Story*. New York: HarperCollins, 1992.

Teilhard de Chardin, Pierre. *Building the Earth*. New York: Avon Books, 1965.

———. *Hymn of the Universe*. N.Y.: Harper & Row, 1961.

———. *The Human Phenomenon*, ed. and trans. Sarah Appleton-Weber. Brighton: Sussex Academic, 1999.

Tillich, Paul. *Biblical Religion and the Search for Ultimate Reality*. Chicago: University of Chicago, 1955.

———. *The New Being*. New York: Scribners, 1955.

———. *Systematic Theology* I. Chicago: U. of Chicago, 1951.

Wilber, Ken. *A Theory of Everything*. Shambhala, 2001.

———. *The Eye of the Spirit: An Integral Vision for a World Gone Slightly Mad*. Boston: Shambhala, 1997.

———. *The Marriage of Sense and Soul*. New York: Random House, 1998.

———. *Sex, Ecology, Spirituality: The Spirit of Evolution*. Boston: Shambhala, 1995.

The Authors

John P. Cock has published five books and leads spirit journey retreats with people of all backgrounds. He and his family spent three decades facilitating community-leadership development and spirit awareness in the United States, Australia, Indonesia, Malaysia, and India.

Lynda L. Cock has taught all age groups around the world: in Alabama, Atlanta, Chicago ghettos and suburbs, Canberra, Jakarta, villages of India, and now teaches at Jesse Wharton School in Greensboro, North Carolina.

Both are program facilitators with the Institute of Cultural Affairs, a group inspired by Joseph Mathews, and the Center for Ecozoic Studies, a group inspired by Thomas Berry.

Cover Designer

Artist **Alex McKeithen** describes his design: "The collage attempts to invoke a spirit of creation, a sense of cosmic intermingling." He is a Davidson College graduate, a student of design and typography in Arnhem, NL, and now teaches graphic design at the State University of New York (FIT).

www.ingramcontent.com/pod-product-compliance
Lightning Source LLC
Chambersburg PA
CBHW051757040426
42446CB00007B/408